THE POWER OF BELIEF

THE STORY OF AN AFRICAN GHETTO CHILD

YUSUF SABIKU

AuthorHouse™ UK
1663 Liberty Drive
Bloomington, IN 47403 USA
www.authorhouse.co.uk
UK TFN: 0800 0148641 (Toll Free inside the UK)
UK Local: 02036 956322 (+44 20 3695 6322 from outside the UK)

Because of the dynamic nature of the Internet, any web addresses or links contained in this book may have changed
since publication and may no longer be valid. The views expressed in this work are solely those of the author and do
not necessarily reflect the views of the publisher, and the publisher hereby disclaims any responsibility for them.

Any people depicted in stock imagery provided by Getty Images are models,
and such images are being used for illustrative purposes only.
Certain stock imagery © Getty Images.

This book is printed on acid-free paper.

ISBN: 979-8-8230-8218-1 (sc)
ISBN: 979-8-8230-8217-4 (e)

Print information available on the last page.

Published by AuthorHouse 04/25/2023

authorHOUSE®

Contents

ACKNOWLEDGMENTS

I would like to praise God for giving me the wisdom and inspiration to write this book. I also express my heartfelt gratitude to all who have made immense contributions in the noble course of writing this book. Some believed in the idea and contributed their valuable time, advice, materials, and finances, which have consequently enabled me to climb the ladder of success all the way to the top.

Their support, in kindness and material generosity, has seen me through thick and thin and eventually catapulted me to where I am today. If not for their unwavering support, articulating the evolution of my humble life journey through this creative account and collection of thoughts aimed at positively empowering and impacting the lives of others might have been impossible, particularly for the youth who equally aspire to achieve big things.

I extend my heartfelt thanks to Malawian journalist and friend, Howard Mlozi, for editing the manuscripts of this book. I also applaud my martial arts teacher, Walter Grahams (Grandmaster Nd'o), for the profound inspiration that fuelled my desire and showed me the passionate way to become a real man. His teachings propelled me to levels I could only imagine.

I also give special mention to Joel Osteen, whose publications have provided me with great insight and inspiration throughout my life. With the knowledge acquired, I realise God gave me and everyone else unique abilities that, if put to good use, might help us become better versions of ourselves.

Undiluted appreciation should also go to my brother, Jabu (aka JB), for being a wonderful training partner. He has helped me realise my dreams.

Big thumbs up to my parents for showing me unfailing love and care by giving birth to me, as well as raising me and nurturing my dreams. The norms and values of life they taught me were just incredible and remain unadulterated to date!

I extol my wife, Memory, and our children for being my greatest fans and companions throughout the best part of my life. Memory, you are my special woman who has been my greatest support system. May God continue to bless you abundantly.

Mr. Tony Karim should as well be commended for his presence every time I needed a pull or push. He has helped me generously and unconditionally to grow mentally, physically, and financially.

To all my relatives and friends: bravo to you! You are simply the definition of that extraordinary extended family who epitomise the proverb "It takes a village to raise a child". No words can sufficiently express my gratitude for the unwavering support you have given me throughout my life.

I would also like to thank Daniel Chaweza, who gave his heart and time to meticulously edit the book, carefully going through every page with such passion and great attention to the minutiae of the book's soul.

May God bless you all!

INTRODUCTION

The potential that exists within us is by far limitless and untapped. It can transform our lives, if we can effectively mingle it with strong beliefs, hard work, devotion, and determination to embrace our passion, thoughts, and actions. *The Power of Belief*, in its simplest term, is a solid foundation for pursuing and fulfilling our dreams, goals, and aspirations no matter the circumstances. It is a natural process that is driven by your powerful, innate desire to achieve excellence, regardless of what people say about you or what society expects from you. *The Power of Belief* provides you with a framework of knowledge on how we can attain fulfilment in our lives.

The Power of Belief simply puts you or prepares you into a forward-gear disposition towards your goals, dreams, or aspirations. It gives you the guts to challenge limitations that are influenced by social, academic, economic, or cultural factors. This book should be used as a roadmap to your success and your voyage to self-discovery. It should be used as a guide to how you can become a better person. This book seeks to appeal to people from all walks of life, especially young people who are faced with a myriad of challenges, including limitations due to various factors, such as poverty and geography. The elaborate philosophical details and principles I acquired from my martial arts teacher are shared throughout.

I have written this book to instil a positive mindset in people and lead them towards self-discovery, particularly those with an insatiable thirst to improve their lives. I am grateful to have this opportunity to present you with *The Power of Belief*, which I hope will be invaluable in your lives. If you, esteemed readers of this book, can properly apply the shared principles and experiences, surely your lives will never be the same. You will improve in different areas, including critical thinking and problem solving. Possibility thinking is the commonest, grandest ingredient in successful people and therefore a secret to a progressive life.

I am a shining example of the *Power of Belief* as far as my career in martial arts is concerned. I was able to embrace self-confidence and repurpose my life out of despair to evolve into a martial artist who is a force to be reckoned with.

Compounded by hopelessness in a poverty-stricken family while living in the slums (ghetto), where the dreams of many youths were shattered, I came to realise that the power of belief is a reflection of one's thoughts. The way we think affects the world around us. That is, if we can only change our mindset and embrace positive thinking, we can free ourselves from the mental shackles of negativity and become empowered to effect change around us.

A belief based on a success-oriented mindset does not know the boundaries of success or what failure looks like. It transforms the mind to be progressive and unstoppable! Furthermore, belief sees opportunities where others cannot, capitalises on problems, and turns them into success stories. Therefore, belief is results-oriented because it strives to achieve success.

Although belief is a really well-known subject, it is embraced by few people who are willing to take the initiative in order to see a change in their different spheres of life. Therefore, belief can make things happen; in this case, it is termed belief oriented success system (BOSS). Embrace the BOSS within you today!

Belief can be defined as confidence in the truth, the existence or reliability of something, without absolute proof that one is right in doing so. From a biblical perspective, belief refers to having a firm or wholehearted conviction or persuasion to regard the existence of God as a fact. Upon comparison of the above definitions of belief, we can see unity between man and his faith in God.

Indeed, God has blessed us with abundant potential to explore different opportunities. He has the supernatural powers to preordain destinies for everyone and wants us to achieve greatness. However, without believing in ourselves and His capabilities, we can hardly see a grain of success in our lives. Therefore, a belief that entirely depends on God is optimistic rather than pessimistic.

God created us, His children, in His own image, and His intentions for us are good. He does not want us to suffer but, in his grace, to be blessed with abundant resources, traceable destinies, and unimaginable greatness. We were created not to be defeated by the pressures of this world, live mediocre dreams, or suffer inferiority complexes because of certain worldly circumstances.

No! Rather, we are created to succeed and overcome any obstacle that stands in our way, only if we believe. To a great extent, what a person believes to be possible or impossible, visible or invisible, audible or inaudible, clear or blurred, determines what he or she can or cannot do. This is the case, because the mind has the power to control the destiny or destination of a person.

This underscores the power of the mind, which is capable of controlling a person to either attain all that he or she needs, or fail. It is, therefore, imperative to possess a great deal of belief and positivity in our thoughts and then seek proper steps to achieve our aspirations. Above all, we should visualise what we need, because it is through visualisation that our dreams can be realised efficiently and effectively.

God is good to us all, but we have a role to play for Him to act on. We should make an effort to have progressive thoughts that should be followed by relevant action because faith without action is in vain. Once again, nothing can happen in our lives without belief and action. Therefore, our beliefs should be firm and a driving force to undertake necessary actions towards achieving our goals, dreams, and aspirations. Remember, belief initiates and affirms the body's actions, a personal conviction towards the completion of certain tasks. Belief is the foundation upon which human excellence is built. The stronger our belief, the further and higher we will go.

ABOUT THE AUTHOR

I come from a large family of eight, consisting of five males and three females. I am the third son and fifth child overall. We lived in one of the most densely populated areas of Lilongwe, Malawi, which presented several challenges while growing up. Due to our financial situation, I faced various limitations, such as inadequate access to basic needs.

Despite the challenges, martial arts remained a significant part of my life. I had a deep passion for it from a young age, and through hard work and dedication, I achieved a 4th-degree black belt. This accomplishment ignited a spark in me, and I decided to open my martial arts school to motivate and inspire others.

Later on, this same spark drove me to pursue a career in the British Army and I excelled in every aspect of my duties, from basic training to advanced combat techniques.

Now, I reside in the United Kingdom, reflecting on my journey and the experiences that have shaped me. I hope that my story serves as an inspiration to others, showing that with belief, hard work and dedication, anyone can achieve their dreams.

MY FATHER

My father, Alibu Sabiku, is one of my role models despite the difficulties he faced bringing up a large family with no clear income. He walked six kilometres daily to earn a living and provide for us. As the family's breadwinner, he motivated me to work hard to break the cycle of poverty. He is a God-fearing man, a sheikh in Islamic circles, and a peasant farmer and second-hand clothes seller. He still believed he could find a way despite the shortages we faced.

My father is my source of inspiration whom I grew up looking up to. He comes from a mountainous village called Chaoni in Machinga district, in the southern region of Malawi. During his youth, my father enjoyed boxing. He has a track record of knocking out several pugilists. It is from that background that I and some of my brothers got the inspiration to become fighters.

THE POWER OF BELIEF

This *belief* word
Is the magic in this world,
Beyond scepticism and comparison,
It comes through a supernatural season.

These words,
Properly targeted at an angle,
Will never let people fall and tangle;
Rather, it saves them from life's deadly jungle.

These words,
Beyond measure and kilos
Have taken people away from zeros,
Elevating them to higher levels to become heroes.

These words,
Though with little description,
Profoundly, if with a lucid perception,
Lead to abundance and manifestation.

These words,
Articulately engraved,
Shall never make you a slave,
But rather, a good accomplice to your grave.

THE POWER
OF BELIEF

What lies behind us and what lies before us are tiny
matters compared to what lies within us.
—Ralph Waldo Emerson

1

MARTIAL ARTS

Bruce Lee, Donnie Yen, and Jackie Chan were among the most prominent martial artists the world has ever produced. In their prime, they produced a series of action-packed movies and appeared on various TV programs. Their work gained great public acceptance and ostensibly motivated scores of men and women, particularly youth, to develop an interest in martial arts, which shaped their physical, emotional, and mental abilities.

During my childhood in Malawi, most school-going children could skip classes and pack themselves in video stores to watch the latest movies—at the time, few homes had TVs.

Martial arts has grown rapidly in recent years, becoming one of the world's most popular sports. It involves using the body, mind, and soul and has attracted a wide variety of men and women. Due to its curative value, martial arts has been rewarding to its practitioners. Studies suggest that incorporating traditional martial arts into medical care plans can provide a complementary strategy to enhance the efficacy of treatment and promote the overall health of individuals with chronic diseases[1]. As such through Martial Arts, most people have acquired splendid qualities essential to making them more successful in most aspects of life.

Apart from being a means of self-defence, martial arts helps people develop a high degree of personal character, willpower, and self-discipline. Such qualities are profoundly beneficial in many endeavours. Martial arts has generally assisted people to develop attributes that enable them to become better students, businesspeople, athletes, and other things.

As someone who has been on the path of martial arts for many years, I decided to write this book to share my experience with people, especially our youth, on how it can help them discover themselves and bring the best qualities to their lives. While writing this book, I followed concrete steps so that its readers can easily absorb its contents without getting confused. Once read carefully, readers will learn proper success principles, which will help them use their time and efforts fruitfully. Basically, this book encourages readers to realise that with belief, hard work, devotion, and determination, they can do and achieve anything in life.

As a way of encouraging you to have beliefs, which should be coupled with well-designed and clear-cut goals, I came up with the acronym BELIEVE, properly explained in the following paragraphs.

---

[1] Wąsik J, Wójcik A. Health in the context of martial arts practice, Phys Activ Rev 2017, 5: 91-94

B: blessed;

E: enthusiastic;

L: limitless;

I: incomparable;

E: eminence;

V: victory; and

E: enlightenment.

Let me now take you through the thought process behind each word as I perceive it.

BLESSED

Throughout my martial arts training and teaching career, I have observed a commonality in most people; everyone possesses some unique and tremendous abilities within themselves, and we are all blessed with enormous gifts and different talents.

But due to self-doubt, fear, and self-imposed limitations, we fail to harness our power and achieve our goals. While searching for the source of the self within the self, doubt is a common hindrance to our respective dreams. However, the one-billion-dollar question remains: Why do we fail though we are hugely blessed?

God has given us wisdom and talents that can make us succeed in life, and His unlimited favours and blessings surround us. However, the most important thing we must do to achieve our dreams is believing and expecting mighty things will indeed come our way.

We don't fail because we don't have talents or qualifications but because we lack belief and self-confidence. To believe is to be strong. More often than not, doubt clouds our energy to set things in motion. Belief is power.

Consider the words of Marianne Williamson, author of *A Return to Love*,[2] who asserts the following:

> Our deepest fear is not that we are inadequate. Our deepest fear is that we are powerful beyond measure. It is our light, not our darkness, that most

---
2   Marianne Williamson, *A Return to Love* (New York: HarperCollins, 1992).

frightens us. We ask ourselves, who am I to be brilliant, gorgeous, talented, fabulous? Who are you not to be? You are a child of God.

Your playing small does not serve the world. There is nothing enlightening with shrinking so that other people won't feel insecure around you. We are all meant to shine, as children do. We were born to manifest the glory of God that is within us. It is not just in some of us; it is in everyone. And as we let our own light shine, we subconsciously give other people permission to do the same. As we are liberated from our own fears, our presence automatically liberates others.

Too often we underestimate the potential that resides within us. When we are wrapped up in our own doubts and fears, the easiest thing in the world is to overlook all the blessings we already have. Well, the fact is, nothing can stop us from achieving greatness if we believe.

The measure in which one's life is affected is equivalent to the degree of one's doubts. As much as we can use our capabilities to make things happen, we must also rely on God, who gave us excellent potential that can remain incomplete if we do not involve Him in our endeavours.

ENTHUSIASTIC

I am a perfect example of what this book stands for. I have massive testimonies to give regarding countless benefits of the power of belief and what it has done for my life. My ability to believe has always been cemented on enthusiasm. As a child growing up in a very impoverished family and environment, with few to no role models to look up to, I was cramped between the jaws of helplessness, mediocre perceptions, and a weak mindset.

An insatiable curiosity came over me as a child after meeting a martial arts teacher who instilled a hardworking spirit in me beyond any reasonable doubt. He showed me that the key to success lies in patience and perseverance. He taught me humility, which he claimed should be mixed with ambition to achieve something big. I confess that it is God who sent that teacher to me so I might be rescued from the spirit of the inferiority complex that held me hostage for ages.

Growing up in an abusive and fragmented, chaotic environment, poverty might have succeeded against my life, but with vigour and determination, I pressed forward, all the while training my mind not to surrender. I had to keep my head above water to survive that kind of environment.

When it comes to chasing your dreams, it does not matter how slowly you go as long as you don't stop going. For my family, it was a slow and steady exodus, but in the end, we were released from the shackles of poverty.

Meanwhile, one must embrace two things to achieve big in life: 'headwork' and hard work. The two should be inseparable. Generally, every person must decide what type of world he or she wants to live in, which happens either consciously or subconsciously.

Most importantly, we must realise that the potential we tap into in our minds and their results are part of an internal process that begins with belief. That is to say that the price of success is having responsibility for our internal dialogue. Whatever is happening within us will directly come outside. Based on our beliefs, we create success.

I have also learnt that the real horror of 'ghetto life' is not packaged in daily frustrations and deprivations, since such things can be easily overcome if we make the right decisions and follow them through corresponding actions and reprogramming our minds and belief systems. A belief without action is dead and therefore meaningless. The twins of any great accomplishment are headwork and hard work. People are usually crafted by what they believe in.

LIMITLESS

Limitations are inevitable, especially when venturing into a new activity or career or pursuing new goals. Like everyone else, I faced limitations, but I did not allow such challenges to halt my lifelong plans of accomplishing my dreams. I believe nothing can stop us from achieving big things. The sky is not the limit if belief is accompanied by ability and action!

The only thing that can limit a person is his or her own mind. I have passed through different experiences that have taught me lessons, including being able to appreciate that life's output is habitually a direct result of one's own thinking and reasoning. Ninety-five percent of the limiting beliefs in our minds are nothing but lies. Beyond reasonable doubt, the number-one reason the majority of people suffer today is that many believe these lies. If we change these beliefs, we begin to experience inestimable changes.

Napoleon Hill asserts, "You can be anything you want to be, if only you believe with sufficient conviction and act in accordance with your faith"[3]. He says whatever the mind can conceive and believe in is achievable.

---

[3]   Napoleon Hill, *Think and Grow Rich* (New York: TarcherPerigee, Classic Edition 2016).

Generally, our state of happiness is dependent on the quality of our thoughts. Nothing can prevent us from achieving great things—except our own thoughts, which often limit us. My martial arts teacher enunciated that, when the mind is absent, we may have our eyes opened but fail to see; we may have ears but never hear; we may have a tongue yet can't taste what we eat. Truly, our boundaries are merely limitations of the self.

The cultivation of the person depends on the rectification of the mind. Belief to a man is like fuel in a car; belief can drive us to great heights beyond our imagination. That is to say when we believe, we can do much and even better. With faith, we can break all barriers that limit our lives, thereby achieving anything we desire, which is the zeal of life.

In general, success will never just sneak into our way of thinking but will come if we are success-conscious. When we think big, we become big and successful. Positive thinking certainly yields positive results, while negative thinking bears negative fruits that affect our lives and our plans and hinders progress. We should believe big; only then will any outcome we achieve be profound and inestimable.

The size of our success is usually determined by the magnitude of our beliefs. If we formulate trivial goals, then the resultant outcomes would follow, but if we have huge goals our achievements would also be great. Indisputably, what a man achieves or fails to attain is the direct response of his own thinking. The Scriptures say, "As a man thinketh in his heart so is he."[4]

Trust in God and His abilities. God works mysteriously, and we can get what He has for us if we create a firm belief in Him while embracing absolute belief in ourselves. Scripture says, "No weapon formed against you shall prosper, and every tongue which rises against you in judgement you shall condemn"[5]. Rendering you unstoppable, breaking all barricades, and therefore achieving greatness.

INCOMPARABLE

As a prerequisite to the advancement of my martial arts career, my teacher gave me the book *Become a Better You* by Joel Osteen. He insisted I read it. I had mixed reactions to the book. I convinced myself that my teacher was crazy since I hardly noticed a link between that book and martial arts.

---

[4]   *Proverbs 23:7* New King James Version
[5]   *Isaiah 54:17* New King James Version

After reading it, I realised how amazing and captivating it was. It not only moulded me into one of the best martial artists, it changed my life. I was inspired to read everything written by Joel Osteen. The more I did, the more empowered I got and the bigger my faith in God grew. Eventually, the contents of *Become a Better You* encouraged me to train harder and become an outstanding figure in the martial arts world.

Oftentimes, the majority of people fail to maximise their potential, a potential that might enable them to achieve greatness, because they imitate others who consequently suffocate their potential. God created us differently, so one person can be excellent in one thing, yet the same thing might prove difficult for another.

We must never compare our lives with that of others. Beyond doubt and measure is the fact that there is no comparison between the sun and the moon. This is crystal clear, and it should never cross our minds to think otherwise. The sun and the moon don't shine at the same time. Therefore, stop comparing yourself to others, as this will only drain your abilities to experience and maximise your uniqueness.

Author Tamara Kulish said, "The razor blade is sharp but can't cut a tree. The axe is strong but can't cut hair"[6]. In other words, everyone is incomparable and unique according to his or her own purpose. This is the rule of nature as embedded in incomparability, matchlessness, and eminence.

We repeatedly fail to realise our potential because of our own limiting beliefs. Our society, for instance, dictates our actions and behaviours. It often tells us how we should act in the presence of others, courtesy of moral behaviours—it even tells us how we should dress and present ourselves, sometimes dictating what we should be in order to be accepted by society. This can inhibit our chances to evolve and grow beyond our limiting beliefs.

The point is we are all created to live and enjoy the fullness of our lives and not to live defined by others. It is our responsibility to make sure we do not blindly follow and abide by these dictations. Each one of us was born and blessed with distinct abilities. In the same way that my goals, ambitions, dreams, and capabilities can never be like yours, your dreams and aspirations can never be mine.

We must deem our uniqueness as an incomparable aspect given by God, and since we are unique, we must not think we are surpassed by others. You should know there is no one like you and will be no one like you. You should be proud of your uniqueness and embrace

---

[6] https://tamarakulish.com/2020/11/28/the-razor-blade-is-sharp-but-cant-cut-a-tree-the-axe-is-strong-but-cant-cut-hair/

your passion, which may lead to success. Be it at work or at home, you should embrace positive thinking, which will link you to success.

Even if we find ourselves in a difficult situation, we must be determined in order to triumph. In times of opportunity and adversity, we must believe we can achieve success. Success should be the master plan that dominates our thinking. Positive thinking fine-tunes our minds to formulate plans that can produce triumph. On the other hand, a *failure mindset* does the opposite—it makes us think of producing trash.

We must be cautious that, whenever we say we can achieve something (or not), that would simply mean we are confessing what we believe we are capable of doing. Effects of faith help in critical thinking and opening doors of excellence. In fact, no force directs human behaviour more powerfully than belief. *Faith* is our internal representation that governs our behaviours and decides what we can achieve.

EMINENCE

Nineteenth-century philosopher and author John Stuart Mill writes, "one person with a belief is equal to ninety-nine who only have interests"[7]. What we earnestly seek to achieve is determined by our careful thoughts, steps, and preparations taken before engaging in any activity. God created every one of us with special gifts and different personalities. Every one of us has notable features. As such, we must be reminded that certain moments of our lives are better than we think. We must say positive words to ourselves, and say them better than we did before.

The truth is one does not need supernatural intelligence to succeed. Prosperity isn't based on luck; successful people are ordinary folks like everyone else who believe in themselves and their potential. We must believe we can move any mountain that blocks our way.

It is written in Matthew 17:20 - 21, "If you have faith as small as a mustard seed, you will say to this mountain, 'move from here to there,' and it will move; and nothing will be impossible for you"[8]. The scripture specifies that you only need your faith (belief) to be 'small'; it doesn't speak of gigantic faith. However, only a few people believe that they can move mountains with faith. Your belief, regardless of how small it can be, can change your life.

---

[7]   https://medium.com/@steveagyebeyondlifestyle/one-person-with-a-belief-is-equal-to-ninety-nine-who-have-only-interests-b038bd1edda7.

[8]   *Matthew 17:20-21* (New American Standard Bible 1995)

Think of a seed, a very tiny thing in nature. But water, sunlight, and other required nutrients from the soil make it eventually sprout and grow into a big tree. Similarly, we humans have almost everything we need (seeds of greatness) to become our best. This is to say we can surely achieve great things if we believe success is possible for anyone. With faith, it is possible for us to transform impossibilities into possibilities.

It also must be emphasised that faith goes hand in hand with action. This is a chicken and egg question: Which comes first? We must learn to act on the things we want to undertake or achieve. We must not be discouraged by how people view us or react to our ideas or initiatives. Instead, we must be determined and remain focused on positive perceptions of ourselves.

In essence, only people who know who they are and what they would like to achieve can pass any test life throws at them. Above all, it is the desire that lies deep inside our hearts and what we believe in that can move us forward. With belief hidden in our hearts, we can do what others can only dream of or can even do much better than them.

As go-getters, we are mandated to recognise our unique qualities as incomparable and inseparable from God, and as such we should not think we are outsmarted. We should meditate on success rather than failure. Every time we are at work or in the comfort of our homes, we should not waste time thinking about our failures but should occupy our minds with progressive thinking. This is what we call a winning mindset.

VICTORY

God created us as complete human beings, with everything we need. He gave us tools that if properly used can make us attain prosperity. But if the same are neglected or abused, we can end up languishing in abject poverty. The good news is that God is always with us, and we fit nicely into His hands. Nobody against us can prevail.

As someone who has experienced life's fluctuations, I have learnt that with faith we can do great things. Through developing our skills and focusing on wishes we can achieve our goals. Belief and absolute determination can make us progress in different aspects. Belief is an abstract component that triggers the energy to do things.

Essentially, belief is the driving force behind the transformation of intangible ideas into concrete components. It is the belief that has enabled the existence of all possibilities, such as innovations, discoveries, great communities, books, and technology, among others. These esteemed works emanated from simple ideas.

Belief has made many people in organisations, business entities, and great nations win various endeavours. In order to achieve victory, we must understand that life is a cumulative process. Whatever we experience in our day-to-day lives is the accumulation of small decisions and actions we make.

Belief is the key ingredient in successful personalities. Disbelief or doubt is the opposing force that contradicts the purpose of human beings or achievements. When the mind doubts, it consequently begins developing a justification for disbelief. This is to say, when we hesitate, we shall be prone to failure; but if we think of victory, sooner or later we shall prevail.

The point illustrates that belief works to fulfil what has been persistently printed on the walls of our subconscious. Whether positive or negative, all belief manifests as products of our mindset. That is why it is widely accepted that we are a product of our thoughts.

Joel Osteen says, "No matter what our current environment dictates, the truth of the matter shall remain that we can be victors and become the kind of people we were designed to be". We pass through some trying times, but we must be as brave as possible to overcome them since our ability to achieve great things rests inside us and in God's hands.

We must always realise that the Creator has the best plans for us, plans to prosper us, not fail us. He wants to douse us with abundant blessings. It is God's solid and ultimate desire to grow us and take us further than we anticipate. Moreover, God's will is strong and unstoppable to work and manifest great things in our lives, beyond what we have ever imagined.

However, certain things must be given utmost value for us to achieve our wishes with God pushing us on the one hand, while we keep standing, hoping, and believing on the other.

Most importantly, we should cultivate faith in God, who breathes life over our aspirations. The fulfilment of our desires lies in His strength, and He will make us victors. Let us put all our trust in Him because it is where our blessings come from.

To prepare our minds for victory and future possibilities, we should not concentrate on our past mistakes but instead take them as lessons; we should love ourselves, trust our choices, and believe that everything is possible and victory is ours. Truly, our greatest glory as believed by Confucius "is not in never falling, but in rising every time we fall"[9].

---

[9]   https://www.brainyquote.com/quotes/confucius_101164

You will fail at some point in your life, which is just part of the process. But you should always remember: failing does not make you a failure. You will only become one if you quit trying. Victory belongs to the most persevering. What are you going to do to achieve your victory?

ENLIGHTENMENT

What do you know about enlightenment? Why is it important? How can we attain it? Even though enlightenment is such a big word, pregnant with meaning—in its simple terms it can be described as an education that yields understanding and insight, which occurs upon acquisition of knowledge and wisdom. It is a step-by-step process of working out our spiritual self.

According to the teachings of the Buddha, enlightenment is said to be the action or state of attaining or having spiritual knowledge or insight, which frees a person from the cycle of rebirth. Furthermore, Buddhists believe the human life is a cycle of suffering and rebirth, but that if one achieves a state of enlightenment (nirvana), it is possible to escape this cycle forever.

However, according to philosophers, enlightenment is a concept in spirituality, philosophy, and psychology related to achieving clarity of perception, reason, and knowledge[10]. This knowledge dominated Europe in the seventeenth and eighteenth centuries, and it is as the Age of Enlightenment.

It was an intellectual movement that encompassed a range of ideas centred on the value of human happiness and the pursuit of knowledge, believed to be obtained by means of sensible reasoning.

In their contrasts and similarities, the definition and the teachings of the Buddha emphasise one common thing: *knowledge.* Specifically, and without a doubt, it is through knowledge and understanding that we can discover the causes of our ignorance, or man's emergence from self-imposed nonage (ability to use one's own understanding without another's guidance)[11] as believed by great philosopher and central enlightenment thinker Immanuel Kant.

In relation to enlightenment, knowledge becomes prominent in understanding information about various relevant subjects.

---

[10] https://www.bl.uk/restoration-18th-century-literature/articles/the-enlightenment

[11] https://www.k-state.edu/english/baker/english233/Kant-WIE-intro.htm#:~:text=Enlightenment%20is%20man's%20 emergence%20from,own%20mind%20without%20another's%20guidance.

Knowledge is obtained in several ways, such as through experience and study. Such knowledge can be static in one person or passed on to others. It is a well-known fact that enlightenment is undoubtedly a weapon that can save a person from anguish and self-imprisonment of ignorance. Although we all search for enlightenment, not many of us attain or utilise it effectively. Yes, it's true that becoming enlightened may not be an easy task. Nevertheless, the great news is you can still move closer to enlightenment every single day.

There are so many proven ways you can become enlightened, but one sure and remarkable way is by living in the present moment. That is, expanding your understanding of life and the world within and around you. The best part of enlightenment is that it is available for everyone who seeks it. When we acquire knowledge and then encounter challenges, we vehemently understand how to deal with them.

Knowledge is a key that broadens our horizons and highlights our inabilities. Talent is not enough on its own; it should be attached to knowledge and its best application or utilisation.

According to the book *Talent is Never Enough* by American author John Maxwell, "To reach our potential, we must believe in our abilities while being determined to live above average. Failure to reach our potential is tragic."[12]

Belief, time, thought, and a positive attitude can help solve most of the problems we face today. If we amass knowledge and understanding, chances are high that there will be no limitations in different endeavours that we undertake or strive to accomplish. If we constantly develop our minds and attain enlightenment, nothing will limit how far we can go and how much we can achieve.

We must devote ourselves to strenuous efforts, positive thinking, analysis, and measurements to obtain complete and accurate knowledge. Knowledge is the acquisition of ability through experience or study. The knowledge we gain through our day-to-day encounters is critical for a successful life. Apparently, with knowledge, we will never go wrong.

We must always remember that, when we say we can do something or we can't, we are surely demarcating or confessing our limits. Effects of what we can get from such a confession will precisely help in opening doors of excellency or closing them eternally. In fact, there isn't a more powerful force in human behaviour than belief. Our faith is an internal force that governs our intuition and results in action or certain patterns of behaviour which lead us to accomplish or fail tasks.

---

[12]   John C. Maxwell, *Talent is Never Enough* (New York, Nelson Business 2007)

Upon reading Dr Robert Schuller's book *Tough Times Never Last but Tough People Do* one would be stimulated to walk in the path of belief. In part, he says, we must educate ourselves to avoid taking shortcuts when doing things, as doing so might lead to wasted years of study and training but bear no expected results. He adds that people who are too lazy to learn never gain the knowledge; as a result, they weaken their chances of success[13].

Schuller not only emphasises the acquisition of knowledge but also its proper use. Knowledge is one of the surest ways of breaking the shackles of poverty.

Ralph Waldo Emerson says, "Every man is an impossibility until he is born"[14]. According to Emerson, our presence in this world is the availability of vast and limitless possibilities through the acquisition of knowledge.

---

[13]   Robert H. Schuller, *Tough Times Never Last but Tough People Do* (Random house, 1984).
[14]   https://quotefancy.com/quote/893604/Ralph-WaldEmerson-Every-man-is-an-impossibility-until-he-is-born

2

REALITIES
OF LIFE

Life without love is a bird without song. Life without trust is a night without day. Life without faith is a tree without roots. Life without hope is a year without spring. Life without friends is a sun without shade. Life without work is a bloom without fruit.
—William Arthur Ward.

Life is defined in many ways, and some definitions are used every day. Among them, life is as 'An imaginary opponent we tussle against, without weapons but visions'[15]. It is understood that we cannot win life's hassles with any kind of weapons but the engagement of our physical and mental abilities.

However, in order for physical and mental aspects to be effective in fighting our daily battles, they should be supplemented with clear visions of what we intend to achieve. Already written in our minds, there must be a clear roadmap or course of action.

Life provides people with dynamic positive and negative experiences. Scores of people fear meeting challenges, although even difficult moments offer positive facets as they foster learning and develop one's confidence and determination.

Everyone faces their own "Goliath", making them prone to challenging moments. But our role is to become a "David", standing firm and coming out brandishing a slingshot to fight such stumbling blocks.

We may not overcome problems as instantly as David did when defeating the biblical Goliath (1 Samuel 17:42–51 New King James Version), but we should learn to persevere when facing drastic situations until we can finally see the light at the end of the tunnel.

The most important thing is to have patience, because significant battles are often won over time. Life is like a boxing match in which each fighter plays two critical roles: strategically *throwing punches* on the opponent's body parts while *ducking* his *blows*.

One thing to remember is that life is a process that begins at birth and ends on the day we breathe our last. Throughout the process, we must understand that it is not possible to dodge every predicament. Instead, we should use these situations as stepping stones towards achieving great things.

At no time should we accept difficult situations to limit our abilities or make us give up on our dreams. We must rise quickly and strongly when life knocks us down because trials and temptations are part of life. Consequently, they play a crucial role in defining our destiny. Winners are distinguished from losers based on their reactions and attitudes, among other things. Losers don't retry when they fail, while winners build resilience against defeat. They keep trying until they succeed.

---

15   Miyamoto Musashi, *The Book of Five* Rings (Shambhala Publications Inc, 2005)

Time and again, those in pursuit of goals will come face-to-face to a point where, regardless of hard work and trying, nothing works. Sometimes our level of thinking or planning will not be enough. This is to say no matter how hard we might try to remain patient and persistent, the fact remains that some things will never change or work out. However, the only way out in such cases is to welcome change.

Our world does not accommodate people who are stuck in certain patterns of thinking with goals that do not work. It is our responsibility to let go of things that don't work and welcome changes.

As illustrated in the first chapter, we all have what it takes—blessed to be the person we want to be. But we will never reach our greatest potential if we are stuck with unproductive habits. Do you want to be the person who clings to goals and ideas that don't work, forever getting the same results?

On the other hand, life is not about doing what we like most, but rather having minimal enjoyment while enduring more. Growing up in Africa, I learnt of many struggles that people overcome. However, chances of prevailing can be achieved if we focus our minds and ourselves on what we intend to achieve.

Training our minds to be sources of inspiration can help achieve remarkable success. Through that, we can build a better world for the current and future generations since the choices we make every day not only affect only us but the people we relate to as well.

CONTROLLING OUR LIVES

Sound life decisions are somewhat dependent on the levels of education we acquire. Africa can achieve greatness if its people realise the value of education. Former South African president Nelson Mandela once described education in his book titled *Long Walk to Freedom* as a catalyst for personal development. He said education can make a peasant farmer's daughter a doctor, the miner's son head of the mining site, a farm worker's son the president[16]. According to him, the way we use resources at our disposal might distinguish us from others. He also underscored the importance of self-discovery as a vital tool for success.

In his book *Universal Laws of Success and Achievement*, Brian Tracy says all things happen for a purpose. He says behind everything is an effect, and behind every effect, whether

---

[16]   Nelson Mandela, *Long Walk to Freedom* (Abacus; New Ed edition 1995)

voluntary or subconscious, is a specific cause[17]. Generally, nothing happens by chance. There is a reason why we were born in various environments or under certain conditions in this life. Most importantly, certain things happen as lessons. For example, if we live in a hostile environment, the duty lies in our hands to improve that environment and make it habitable for us and others.

Ghanaian single mother Princess UmulHatiyya Ibrahim, in her early thirties, started her journey to success. She was the first African to go on a voyage around the world. Apart from being a traveller, Hatiyya was a banker, an author, entrepreneur, a philanthropist, and founder of PUH foundation, a charitable education organisation focusing on building a first-class Africa. If we are to make Africa great, we have to take control of our own lives and the environment we come from. Above all, we should learn from what others have done.

We should also constantly remind ourselves that all we have become or are about to be is a result of all that we have thought. Meaning; our thoughts will create and control our physical realities through what is called *manifesting*.

Albert Einstein once said, "The significant problems we have cannot be solved at the same level of thinking with which we created them"[18]. All the major problems humans experience today were created by our own thinking.

In order for us to solve most of these problems and be in control of our lives, we must completely change our mindset and trust in the magic of thoughts. The power to change our environment lies within us; we are masters of our situations. That is, the power of belief determines whether we are set to solve our situations or exacerbate them.

---

[17]   Brian Tracy, *Universal Laws of Success and achievement (Nightingale-Conant, 2014)*
[18]   https://www.goodreads.com/quotes/272021-the-significant-problems-we-have-cannot-be-solved-at-the

3

DISCOVER WHO YOU ARE

Our lives and the world we live in are but only temporary and in a state of change; one must become one with the self, leading oneself to a realisation of truth and purpose. For only through himself and herself will people be able to discover themselves.
—Author unknown

DISCOVERING YOURSELF THROUGH YOUR SELF

Aristotle stated: "Knowing yourself is the beginning of all wisdom."[19] Perhaps this underscores the power of discovering yourself (knowing who you are). Discovering who you are is a process of identifying your strengths and weaknesses.

How do you handle life? Do you structure your identity around hurts and blows, or do you move on despite your past? Only through introspection of the limits and capabilities of the body, mind, and soul can one truly reach any meaningful sense and cultivation of the self. Knowledge of your true self is prominent and therefore crucial. As a matter of fact, it is more imperative for one to know his own self than it is to know another.

People make the mistake of trying to discover themselves through others, yet the only way they can discover themselves is through themselves—by knowing who they really are. Confucius said, "What the superior man seeks is in himself; what the small man seeks is in others". As you walk through the path to self-discovery, do not look for the *self* in others; preferably, seek the self within you.

Trying to cultivate your true self through another's self is like trying to cram a size ten foot into a size one shoe. Attempting to employ somebody else's realisation of their self as your own only leads to frustration. It also leads to *Maya*, or a false image as referred to by Hindus. Once you discover your true self, it is possible to discover anything else.

In a real sense, it is the obligation of every person to understand themselves better than seeking the truth and insight from another self. We can discover ourselves by improving, understanding, and mastering our old selves, thereby choosing and willing to have a new self.

Personally, martial arts training has helped me in a tremendous number of ways. Among the notable benefits is the ability to discover my real identity (self!).

In the course of discovering the *self* through my abilities, I have mastered the actual self in me. Now I perceive myself as the real SELF (shapeless, effortless, limitless, and formless). What lies outside every form is a manifestation of the self that lies within. Without the self there is no life, and without life there is no form. We must strive to discover ourselves through our real self.

---

[19]   https://www.haystalentsolutions.com/-/-knowing-yourself-is-the-begining-of-all-wisdom-aristotle

MARTIAL ARTS AS A WAY OF DISCOVERING THE SELF

Martial arts is a set of combat skills practiced in China, Japan, Korea, and other countries. For a long time, people perceived the art negatively. For instance, some associated it with violence and pride. However, the misconception is gradually fading with the emergence of a new generation spearheading the art. Martial arts is a tough sport yet physically, emotionally, and spiritually rewarding.

Essentially, it does not train people to fight; instead, it helps them develop much-needed skills and techniques to curb problems they face daily. Whether we live as martial artists or non-martial artists, we all face challenges. The sport is there to help us emerge victorious.

Martial arts is usually misinterpreted, as some people deem it a harmful, warring, and fighting sport. On the contrary, martial arts encourages strong-mindedness and critical thinking in addressing challenges as one pursues his or her wishes. It is well known that martial arts fosters the cultivation of positive perceptions in people towards life, through the creation of a progressive mindset, belief in the self, and a hardworking spirit, which are key in overcoming confrontations and solving problems. Martial arts training is not only designed for self-protection but for self-perfection.

Just like most things we do, the acquisition of martial arts skills is a gradual process that requires patience, hard work, and resilience. Like babies who learn how to crawl and then to walk, we also pass through stages in martial arts. There is absolutely no challenge that can outsmart a person who can conquer him or herself. We can become efficient in martial arts if we perfect our spiritual, physical, mental, and emotional components.

Students pursuing martial arts are trained to take a larger view of life. The fusion of mind and action is the ultimate test for martial artists. To the individual, the skill amalgamates discipline, physical, and spiritual moral forces. We can only be true martial artists if we are people of good deeds that are complemented by hard work and determination.

For a person to become a splendid martial artist, one must excel at releasing powerful punches and fast kicks. One must also remember that the value of living a virtuous life is of paramount importance. And one should be of good character by desisting from any acts of violence and aggression.

DISCOVERING THE SELF THROUGH POSSIBILTY REASONING

Martial artists should do things with religious intent. They should make sound decisions centered on reasoning, which might help them understand themselves. Every martial artist and non-martial artist should answer some pertinent questions, such as

- Who am I?
- Where am I coming from?
- How did I get here?
- Where do I want to go?
- How can I get there?

The importance of these questions is that the responses obtained might help discover oneself. I once asked myself the same questions, and my answers facilitated my journey of self-discovery.

The impact of martial arts on the world is immense. Among valuable contributions, it has helped people living in the Western world develop much-improved mindsets.

Purified mindsets have been introduced to African countries through books and movies. Though there are countless misconceptions attached to martial arts, the sport has struck a responsive chord in my life and in the lives of other Africans through experience, belief, and self-discovery.

Most Africans have a tendency to look down on themselves, so much that they think they cannot achieve anything positive or great. The absence of self-confidence and self-realisation and an abundance of anxiety, emotional instability, tension, and physical and mental ailments are the cause of poor societies. Throughout my martial arts career, I have seen the expansion of my concentration levels with the assimilation and application of my skills. Fundamentally, the effect of martial arts skills on my life is more prominent than other lessons I have learnt. It has assisted me in having a positive outlook on issues.

WATER AS AN ELEMENT OF THE SELF

Calm, like that of still waters, is an important element of the self. Core elements of martial arts training are established in training the body and mind. A calm mind can take us a long way. Martial arts not only influences our thoughts and lifestyles, it helps us discover the *self*.

While applying principles of martial arts in our everyday lives, we must strive to be as natural and calm as water. We must be inquisitive to understand martial arts fundamental principles. We must strive to be clear with issues taught while refusing ignorance to interfere with our enlightenment. When practising martial arts, we should aim at harmonising the body and the mind. This process is called the harmony of yin and yang.

Bruce Lee's book, *Tao of Jeet Kune Do,* describes martial arts competitions as swimming on dry land[20]. Lee believed martial artists should be spontaneous and unpredictable, as one is only required to react to it. He says well-versed martial artists should flow fluidly and without hesitation, like water.

Lee borrowed the belief from Chan Buddhism, which says "Martial arts should flow freely like water being poured from a cup"[21]. Lee's philosophy talked of casting off what is useless[20]. He compared it to a sculptor's mentality, who, when moulding his images, begins with a simple lump of clay. He then removes all non-essential elements for the best creation only. He therefore said, in martial arts, one should struggle to remain with the best combat essentials.

Lee emphasised that we face various situations in a fight and in life, but to overcome them we should not be rigid in our ways of dealing with them. Instead, we must flow freely like water. Lee's philosophy—which says we can easily overcome situations if we flow like water—is a good one.

Generally, the philosophy emphasises that whenever we are cornered with situations, we must be flexible and open minded to face them like water, which takes the shape of the container it is in. Each of us has streams of unlimited potential flowing and waiting to be tapped, but we can achieve these potentials only if we are fearless and selfless.

Lee's theory further says that we must function properly in any situation and react to it accordingly[22]. One should know when to speed up or slow down. We must know when to expand and when to contract, or when to flow and when to crash.

It is only through awareness that life and fighting can be shapeless and ever-changing, which can allow us to adapt them. Lee did not believe in 'styles'; he felt that every person and situation are different and not everyone can fit into them. We must remain flexible to

---

[20]   Bruce Lee, *Tao of Jeet Kune Do* (Black Belt Books, 2011).
[21]   https://goodreads.com/quotes/9053219-empty-your-mind-be-formless-shapeless-like-water-now-you
[22]   https://goodreads.com/quotes/9053219-empty-your-mind-be-formless-shapeless-like-water-now-you

obtain new knowledge and victory. Our minds should never be rigid, including dealing with situations; we must evolve and move towards improving ourselves.

Bruce Lee also said he made sure he learnt something new in every situation. He said the same should be done by everyone. Lee said we should not go out and look for successful personalities but stressed that we should start from the root of our lives and see how we can accomplish what we see in other people. Martial artists should believe in the meaning and importance of their actions.

True martial artists have attained mastery of living and think outside the box. They use limitations as a means of reaching their goals. They have open minds towards nature.

UNDERSTANDING THE SELF

Upon acquiring physical strength, one's attitude towards life should change completely; it must focus on possibilities and pursue the existence of a tranquil and unfettered mind. The state of peaceful co-existence between the body and mind can be achieved only after vigorous training.

Each training stage is based on a deeper understanding and development of the self. With a consistent training routine, we can improve in doing things we considered extremely difficult previously. What we might take simple and for granted today, could be among the things we considered impossible yesterday. With vigorous training, we can overcome what is impossible and then become possible and achievable.

Improvising, adapting, and overcoming (IAO) are the ingredients that make up a successful life. The type of life we might lead is simply a reflection of our thoughts, actions, and hard work. Emerson said, "The ancestor of every action is a thought"[23]. Just like an echo, life gives back every single bit we give it. Most people fail to realise that the fruits of their efforts vary according to their levels of thinking, hard work, and determination. This means that the quality of life we lead is a result of efforts and commitment, regardless of what we choose to do. It is a common fact that people who do nothing can achieve nothing as well since our life stories are not written with pens but with actions.

Japanese philosopher Miyamoto Musashi warns that it is impossible to become experts in a particular field or achieve our goals overnight. He says our minds should first be prepared for a particular task and that forcing matters usually leads to failure. According to him, life is an imaginary opponent that cannot be confronted with weapons but visions. He

---

[23]   https://medium.com/@ankushskapoor/the-ancestor-of-every-action-is-a-thought-ralph-waldo-emerson-8593e43650c8

explains that life is a fight between the protagonist and antagonistic forces that call for our understanding of a series of lessons[24].

IMPROVING THE SELF

A good martial artist must be physically strong and mentally and spiritually sturdy because all techniques involved are based on movements of the body and proper usage of the mind. The combination of mind, body, and soul is developed at the initial stage of the art but should be refined regularly. The coordination of techniques used in martial arts can hardly be achieved without combining the body, mind, and soul. It is through this combination that martial artists are connected to all aspects of human nature. Martial artists should remember that success means shifting from failure to failure without losing belief and enthusiasm. Martial artists should strive to attain excellence not only in the art but in other aspects of life. Just as a spark of fire can lead to intense heat, effectiveness in improving the self is also dependent on the magnitude of efforts we employ.

For us to become what we have always wanted to be, there is a need for us to search deep within ourselves and awaken the giant to allow the seeds of our dreams, inner exploration, and outer printing to occupy a larger space in our lives. Generally, our future is determined by the type of seeds we sow today. We must sow belief today and harvest abundant fulfilment tomorrow.

MASTERING THE SELF

The level of personality and character we can attain depends on the amount of effort we exert. Life is dependent upon hard work and diligence. While traveling on the path of mastering the self, we should live as warriors and expect a lot of things to happen on that journey.

However, one disheartening thing is that some of the problems that block our way are a result of our own thinking. We must realise that our thoughts determine what we can and cannot achieve. Some people look at themselves as failures when compared with others. *Worriers* stay defeated, but *warriors* do not remain down on the battlefield; rather, they fight back regardless of the circumstances.

We should not allow problems to dictate our lives but embrace them as part of our lives. Tussle against negative thinking and then cultivate a positive attitude even in the middle of great despair.

---

24   Miyamoto Musashi, *The Book of Five Rings* (CreateSpace Independent Publishing Platform, 2012)

There is a common thread that runs through the lives of people who cannot see any light at the end of the tunnel when they are knocked down. But every time we are knocked down, we must swiftly rise. The choice to give up or carry on is a defining moment. (Martial artists can refine their self through the cleansing of their skills via practice.)

Giving up is a tragedy. The choice is simple; we can decide to stand up and be counted or lie down and be ignored. Defeat never comes to people until they accept it. In other words, defeat is a choice made by an individual whether to accept it or not. So never accept defeat as your ultimate choice. *Never!*

Our attainment of the self will be measured by our willingness to keep trying. Defeat is not when we stumble or fall but when we surrender to the situation. Nothing can keep us down unless we decide not to rise again. Frankly speaking, failure in a person is not registered with defeat but with the decision to give up.

True warriors are people who master the art of living. Warriors should be decisive. As the saying goes: "Every arrow that hits the bull's eye is a result of one hundred misses". We must be determined to fight a battle several times to win it. Just because we were once defeated should not be used as an excuse to give up or look down on ourselves. Rather, it should be used as motivation to train harder and do better next time.

Always remember that the principle of persistence entails that we should never stop trying. "Defeat is a state of mind, no one is defeated until the crush has been accepted as a reality".

In times of pessimism and lacking confidence when we are defeated, do not listen to the voices of the defeated mental self. To master the self, we must be like warriors. Our greatest enemy is inside us.

Japanese martial artist Morihei Ueshiba said, "There are no contests in the art of peace, and a true warrior is invisible because he contests with nothing, yet failure means to defeat the mind of contention that is harboured within"[25].

The way of mastering the self involves what is called the 3Ds: dedication, determination, and devotion. This also constitutes the formula for success: belief + hard work + devotion + determination = success. The more we believe and act in accordance with our faith, the sooner it becomes our second nature and acted in the desired way. We can do anything or be anyone we wish if we learn to believe in ourselves. With belief, we can reach our highest potential.

---

25   https://www.pinner-aikido.com/en/aikido/articles/morihei-ueshibe-quotes-94

When we feel a down, consider the inspiring words created by Edgar Albert Guest in the 1920s[26]:

"Don't Quit"

You're trudging seems all uphill,
When the funds are low, and the debts are high
And when you want to smile but you must sigh,
When care is pressing you down a bit,
Rest, if you must – but don't quit.

Life is queer with its twists and turns,
As every one of us sometimes learns,
And many a fellow turns about when he might
When he might have won, had he stuck it out,
Don't give up, though the pace seems slow
You might succeed with another blow

Success is failure turned inside out,
The silver tint of the clouds of doubt,
And you can never tell how close you are,
It may be near when it seems far.
So, stick to the fight when you are hardest hit,
It's when things get worse that you mustn't quit!

While working on improving the self, we must also not undermine the importance of knowledge. There are two ways to acquire knowledge: formally and informally. Education is believed to be a trusted form of acquiring knowledge. In his book *Emotional Intelligence*, Daniel Goleman says academic intelligence has some gaps, including its failure to help people recognise opportunities[27].

Honestly, outside the classroom, something more than qualifications is crucial. It is enshrined in the ability to think big and embrace enthusiasm and persistence, especially when we encounter setbacks.

John Mason, author of *Imitation Is Limitation* says people who are timid always do too little[28]. It is possible that we can achieve a lot in our lives, but the key is to try doing the

---

[26] https://www.thepeoplesfriend.co.uk/2020/05/24/dont-quit-an-inspiration-poem-by-edgar-a-guest/

[27] Daniel Goleman, *Emotional Intelligence* (Bloomsbury Publishing PLC, 1996).

[28] John Mason, *Imitation is Limitation* (Orient Paperbacks, 2010)

impossible. Under any circumstances we must believe in ourselves, because if we don't, we create barriers to our own triumphs.

The only thing perceived as standing between most people and their dreams is the fear of failure, which encourages self-limitations to take root. We must break that cycle and seek to go beyond self-imposed barricades and fear of the unknown.

However, failure is a result of not having the courage to try things out, nothing more nothing less. As well observed and approved, failure is an essential element to success in any endeavour of life. Apart from its agonising pain, failure tests us, yet on the same note, it also offers us the lessons for growth and guidance along the path of mastering the self. The science of failure is that like any other creation, it is our own creation. Never fear failure, embrace it with open arms and a positive mentality to learn from it.

4

KNOWLEDGE AS AN ASPECT OF ACHIEVING OUR DREAMS

What matters most is not how much you have learned but how much you have absorbed in what you have learned.
—Bruce Lee

Most people have the desire to achieve significant success. Be it mentally, physically, or spiritually, almost everybody wants to be great to attain satisfaction. To achieve that, desire alone is inadequate; a plethora of knowledge in the form of willingness, effort, and hard work must be added.

WHAT IS KNOWLEDGE?

Knowledge is the ability to obtain information through experience, reasoning, or acquaintance. Knowledge is defined as the understanding of information about a subject that a person gets through experience or study.

Knowledge is not limited to the place one comes from but what one eagerly seeks. Whether we are from the Caribbean, Asia, Africa, or Europe—rich or poor, black or white—the fact is, we all require knowledge. Regardless of our circumstances, knowledge will help make us successful, breaking all barriers and limitations within and around us. Specifically, like knowledge, success has no limits; it is only through our perception and lack of knowledge that we begin to experience limitations.

The reason many people don't achieve what they want is that their knowledge of success is limited. It is also the same reason most people in Africa and other parts of the world perceive themselves as inferior, partly because of the values and limitations that are imposed on them, which is the direct result of a knowledge gap.

This condition automatically deprives them of self-confidence to undertake certain significant actions or moves in order to improve their lives.

The secret is, if we learn to embrace and utilise knowledge effectively, regardless of our present status quo, our reality will never be the same. Surely there will be a triumph at the end of the day.

Though knowledge is important, we should also be mindful that its utility requires taking appropriate steps. It requires personal effort, such as critical thinking, to be able to analyse it and grasp what is important and applicable to our scenario. Many people are knowledgeable yet still struggle. Generally, the key role of information is to unlock doors to our success.

Plutarch remarked, "The richest soil, if uncultivated, produces the rankest weeds". Possession of great skill and vast knowledge alone cannot help us thrive if we don't have the desire to take action. We should cultivate strong willpower coupled with the right knowledge if we want to make an impact. In general, a strong desire is the fuel that drives our ambitions.

HOW TO ACQUIRE KNOWLEDGE

The foundation of excellence is built on solid and well-defined knowledge. Acquisition of complete, accountable, and accurate knowledge requires devotion to strenuous efforts, analysis, and measurement. Be aware also that, as Confucius said, "Learning without thought is labour lost; thought without learning is perilous". This means we should learn from daily encounters and powerful books, the knowledge that can foster our victory. With vast knowledge, the world surely cannot limit us, unless God decides to set boundaries for our lives.

There really should be no end to learning. It is not that you read a book, pass an exam, and then you finish learning. The whole of your life, from the moment you are born to the moment you die, is a process of learning, a process of seeking knowledge and a better understanding of the world around you. As humans, we tend to react to certain situations by making well-informed choices when we have knowledge because knowledge is power!

THE VALUE OF KNOWLEDGE

As far as success is concerned, knowledge is of critical importance in various ways, including

• Knowledge makes us valuable

When one has knowledge and skills other people don't have, that person is valued and respected regardless of his or her appearance or where he or she comes from. With knowledge comes an increased ability to do things in your life you never dreamed possible.

• Knowledge helps us discover our potential

Knowledge helps us overcome situations some people deem difficult and insurmountable. In teaching his disciples, Confucius once said, "Real knowledge is to know the extent of one's ignorance". When one understands something he did not understand, one becomes well-informed, hence acquiring knowledge. He further states that, when seeking knowledge, we must learn as if we are not reaching our goals and as though we were scared of missing them.

CREATIVITY AND INNOVATION

If we dream to attain noteworthy success in life, we must be willing to innovate.

Creativity is the state of mind that allows one to have a lot of ideas and be ready to implement them to bring forth tangible results.

Creativity is especially expressed in the ability to make connections and associations, to turn things around, and to express them in new ways.

Creativity is being able to accept truths and think differently so we can do what nobody else has done. The reason most people do not achieve their goals is that they fail to come up with unique ideas.

Our mental, physical, emotional, and spiritual states are a result of our thoughts, as stated in the book of Proverbs 23:7, which says, "For as he thinketh in his heart, so is he"[29]. Through that scripture we can learn that we should be creative to achieve long-lasting results.

Usually, whatever people can see in us starts with our level of thinking. Creativity is of paramount importance in such a competitive world. Creative skills are not a bonus but a necessity. Not everyone can be equally creative, but it is necessary for each of us to learn a skill.

Growing up in an African environment, I realised that most people fail because they lack creativity and an enabling environment to showcase or monetise their skills. Most systems, including education, do not value people's talents but intelligence (IQ), which is easily quantified. For instance, our education system pushes us to blindly follow others—and does not teach us life's fundamentals. The current system has viciously corrupted our minds and will neither help us find our purpose, achieve our dreams, or teach us how to create strong foundations.

This has a negative impact on leadership styles that continue to look at IQ as the only measure of excellence at the expense of other equally important elements of personal development, such as emotional intelligence (EQ), which fosters talents. There is an urgent need for African leaders to change their mindset and respond to the needs of the modern world, which requires several pieces, including creativity and innovation, to solve the puzzle.

---

[29] *Proverbs 23:7 King James Version*

As a result of failed systems of government leaders tend to leave their subjects desperately trapped in the jaws of poverty, which has been a cause of pain and suffering for a long time. It is high time Africa rethinks its ways of doing things and starts nurturing talents among its people. Africa must embrace creativity and innovation if it is to achieve big things on the developmental front.

THE ON AND OFF SWITCHES OF LIFE

Switch on: an act that describes a way of starting the flow, operation of something by means of a tap, switch, or button. This action requires turning on—putting on and starting a process[30]. It is commonly used in the military but it bears a different meaning. In the military, when one is considered 'switched on', it means that the individual is very mindful and aware of his or her intended activities. Just like certain machines need a button to be switched on. Similarly, with life, we were all born with an invisible switch, flipped on the day we are born and off the day we depart, as decided by the creator himself.

ON LIFE

The inspiring and breath taking words of Abraham Lincoln (the sixteenth president of the United States) were well articulated: "That some achieve great success is proof to all that others can achieve it as well"[31]. Mr Lincoln's words give us the awareness to believe that Malawi and Africa, as a whole, with decisive actions and commitment, can change and become economically independent.

If countries like China, Japan, and India made it, what can stop Malawi or Africa from making it too? I strongly believe we can make a better Malawi if we commit ourselves and learn from the past as well as how other countries are doing.

It is a fact that a producing and exporting country is likely to achieve significant economic growth. Malawi, just like other countries, can become a producing and exporting country too. What is required is a mindset change and systematic steps to take.

Agriculture is the economic backbone of Malawi. She has strategic commodities, such as tea, Kilombero rice, tobacco, and the newly approved farming of industrial hemp, which, if properly managed and packaged, can turn around the economy of this country.

Drawing lessons from neighbouring countries Zambia, Tanzania, and Zimbabwe can also help Malawi make economic strides. For example, if we uphold and restore our

---

[30]   Definition from Oxford Languages, https://languages.oup.com/google-dictionary-en/
[31]   https://www.brainquote.com/quotes/abraham_lincoln_385457

cultural values amongst our societies, not only will we bring change, but togetherness as well as a nation. By embracing change and acting decisively, we can attain incalculable accomplishments.

It is well known that if we want to get to the top, we must emulate the highest achievers. As a nation, who do we use as an example? What are we doing that will palpably change us?

By adapting considerable and analysed systems of government in Malawi, as a result of learning from other countries ways, we will benefit ourselves. Hence, the realisation of our nation's growth. Why can't we learn from China's predicament? Now, if you take a moment to think and reflect around you, you will see that certain things needing to be changed and eradicated are holding you or someone back. But we must ask ourselves, who are we waiting for and directing these problems to? I believe it is the responsibility of our nation to make sure such rectifications are carried out.

ON PRODUCTIVITY

Several reasons have contributed to our nation's dilemma Some of those lessons, as I've come to discover, is the tendency of most Malawians to 'switch off their heads (thinking)', mostly from Friday night until Sunday night. Then they switch on again on Monday morning, returning from the weekend filled with petty and trivial conversations brought to our workplaces as their preamble. God gives us 86,400 seconds per day, so switching off for two days means 172,800 seconds are wasted. Why should we waste and not invest all these seconds given to us for free?

The product of too much idle and unnecessary time wasting results in a booming population and poverty. Let us all move away from old systems and routines and try something new. This lazy attitude is never going to bring about any better or profound changes to our nation. We all aspire for a good life (surely it is in every person's dream), but being at ease and idle does not necessarily mean switching off. Let's be mindful of the "switch of life", because this switch is on from the moment we are born and off the moment we die. I believe it's our choices that will make us exist in light or slumber of darkness.

President Franklin Delano Roosevelt asserted, "The only limit to our realisation of tomorrow will be our doubts of today"[32]. My mother, Malawi, believed the kind of mentality we've acquired will only hold us hostage, promote feelings of inferiority, and give birth to losers,

---

[32]   https://medium.com/@officialprpatel002/the-only-limit-to-our-realisation-of-tomorrow-will-be-our-doubts-of-today-franklin-d-roosevelt-664b8f0295eb?source=rss-------1

resulting in nothing other than an impoverished nation. Why should we let this become a norm? We cannot afford to accept mediocrity and poverty.

ON EDUCATION

All things considered, Malawi is a strong and hardworking nation. So instead of switching off and allowing negativity and unproductive behaviours to direct us, why can't we meditate on minimising water and electricity problems? We can focus on creativity and innovation for developmental change; reduction of dependency on the pull-down syndrome (a phenomenon where people disparage those who do well); introduction of new and improved irrigation systems; better health and safety measures; efficiency in production; and changing and nurturing mindsets to resolve the escalation of unemployment and poverty levels. Above all, it means improving the quality of our education systems. Generally, this includes our political, economic, social, and legal environments.

How then do we expect our country and personal lives to improve and expand from this economic turmoil, presumably if all we do is complain and leave everything in the hands of the government? As a matter of fact, the government is occupied with its own agendas and vicissitudes.

Wake up, Malawi! Our country is fifty-eight years old, and it's more than high time we ask ourselves: What are we doing or going to do to bring change to Malawi? Are you an employer or a businessperson creating job opportunities? It doesn't matter what you do as long as it will bring change. It's a question of whether you're going to impact one person or the general public.

ON MORALITY

How will discussing politics or football topics in the workplace positively put us on the world map? Will stealing from our own government make us one of the richest countries in Africa? Will an act of killing innocent people with Albinism give us any good reputation? Will working less efficiently and demanding more make us better people?

It breaks my heart to see fellow Malawians struggling to put food on the table when they work hard to earn a living, or our youth graduating from higher education yet jobless and unprepared for the real world. Malawians who are potentially life changers become displaced when our own country doesn't appreciate their talents and contributions.

On the contrary, it's even more painful to see a grown man playing *Bawo* (a traditional Malawi game where participants use small marbles on a carved wooden board) the whole day for the sake of passing time when another is just as busy but making or initiating change. It's time to wake up, Malawi! We must begin to think about and perceive things on a broader scope. We have all it takes to become a great nation, but our success will never manifest in our narrow and limited mindsets. We've got to change.

As a nation, let's all dig deeply within our souls and digest this: If not us, who? If not now, when? If we can't do it by ourselves—if we don't make Malawi a better place—then who will do it for us? And when will that be?

It will not happen through a miracle. We alone, with proper thinking and undivided efforts, can solve this. You and I have many solutions.

After all these years, we've grown and are still moving forward. Just as a son becomes independent from his parents at a certain age, our time is overdue as a country to keep depending heavily on donor funds. We are surrounded by golden opportunities and untapped resources; if well utilised, we can turn things around. I liken our situation to being like a man dying of thirst yet swimming in freshwater. Why should we live in a land of plenty when we suffer from extreme poverty?

ON DEVELOPMENT

Instead of always asking for funding, we can encourage and embrace a culture of creativity and innovation in Malawi. Creativity and innovation are key elements that will unlock future doors of our economic prosperity and those of other African countries. One common trait about Malawians is that we have lots of ground-breaking ideas, but because we lack creativity and innovation, we die with these ideas, taking them to the grave without implementation. We are so afraid to take risks, and as a result, we fail to realise our potential.

Time and again, people who don't take chances are the ones who never get ahead. If we can educate ourselves and overcome our fears, only then we will be able to take charge of the world around us, because we would be too powerful as a united force. That is also why others work so hard to be where they are.

Leaders encourage our people to venture into SMEs (small- and medium-sized enterprises), which help enhance creativity, resolve high unemployment rates, and contribute to our economic growth. As leaders, your duty is to effectively fulfil your tasks—but many leaders do the opposite.

Why then should we have these people in leadership roles if all they think about is themselves? Leaders who are self-possessed think only of enriching their pockets and bellies while other souls go to sleep on empty stomachs. It's not a matter of how many people serve us in leadership positions; it's about how well they serve. Leadership is about enthusiastically influencing others positively. The ultimate role of a true leader is to serve and not starve others. For goodness sake, we need to change!

Let's love our country and join hands to work towards change. You can do something I cannot do, and I can do something you cannot do—but together we can bring change and make Malawi a better place for us and generations to come.

Chinese philosopher Lao Tzu said, "A journey of a thousand miles begins with a single step". Let's take that step and begin now.

A lot has been said, but little has been done; let's be pragmatic. No more talking—it's action time. Remember, it's not really a question of what to do but having the will to do it. May these words impact you and those who are working meticulously on a good cause in bringing change to Malawi. Let us keep Malawi, as they say, "The warm heart of Africa".

5

THE SEDUCTION
OF SUCCESS

Success is almost totally dependent upon drive and persistence. The extra energy required to make another effort or try another approach is the secret of winning.
—Denis Waitley, author of *The New Psychology of Winning*

Oftentimes I ask myself far-fetched questions, such as When can we say we have achieved success? How much money can one claim in order to be successful? How many gold medals are enough? When is our cup finally full?

To answer these questions, Marlon Brando once said, "It's the hardest thing in the world to accept a 'little' success and leave it that way".[33] Some people say success is like a drug whose effects can be intoxicating, while others relate it to love-making that leaves a person desiring more.

The central message is that managing success is a challenging yet rewarding experience. If done properly, it can shift us from one height to another, enabling us to enjoy the freedom and flexibility it offers. But if neglected we can stagnate, thereby creating a life of chaos and unhappiness.

Essentially, there are no limitations as regards to how much success we can acquire or how far we can go. We should not permit our thoughts to set any limitations. We must always believe and keep growing, and we must not stop learning, because life never stops teaching. Success gives limitless lessons, which must be limitlessly held. Generally, it is our own perceptions that limit us. Essentially, the biggest roadblock to our success is ourselves.

SELF-CONFIDENCE

Self-confidence is defined as being assured of one's personal judgement, power, and ability. Confidence comes from the Latin word *fidere*, meaning *to trust*. Basically, to have self-confidence is to have trust or belief in oneself. Self-confidence is of utmost importance.

Psychologically, people who lack self-confidence may fail or even not try anything, whilst those with a high level of self-confidence may succeed. In short, to have self-confidence is to be aware of your strengths and weaknesses, thereby having a realistic perception of yourself towards anything you attempt.

Some of our forefathers took steps towards doing things the same that we are using today, which was achieved through visions. As members of the current generation, we can create things as our ancient fathers did. We should not be discouraged or brought back when we are side-lined or fail. When such situations come, we must earnestly identify the reasons that led to our predicaments and then realise that there must have been a cause for our failure or the cause for our suffering.

---

[33] https://quotefancy.com/quote/1104490/Marlon-Brando-It-s-the-hardest-thing-in-the-world-to-accept-a-little-success-and-leave-it.

We should not be anxious when we face challenges, for some enter our lives for a reason. Sometimes we might face challenges as a means of testing whether we are in dire need of what we want. Or they might be a life-screening process to measure our levels of resilience and intentions for a particular need.

We need to have confidence that we can improve our lives and that failing or rejection does not necessarily mean we cannot achieve great things.

This can best be illustrated with the following story about a boy who went rock climbing, and what he discovered. While hiking a mountain one particular day, he found an eagle's nest with an egg in it. He took the egg and then headed home. He placed the egg where the chickens laid her eggs. Later, the chicken eggs hatched some chicks while the eagle's egg hatched an eaglet.

Since the eaglet was hatched at the same time as the chicks, it grew along with the chicks, raised by the same hen. The eaglet thought it was the same species as the chicks. Eventually, it learned chicken behaviours. But later, the eagle realised there were some things the chicks could easily do, but it could not manage to do them the same way.

One day an adult eagle flew over the farm, and it happened that the young eagle spotted the flying adult. It had the burning desire to fly high like the adult eagle so that it might fly over mountain peaks. With determination, the young eagle tried to spread its wings to fly, and suddenly it flew higher. That was the time it realised its ability to fly. Though the young eagle had never flown before, it possessed the instinct and capabilities.

The story illustrates that, with confidence and conviction, we can achieve extraordinary things. To become all that we are destined to be, we must be resolute in our actions and never settle for less. Above all, we should have mighty confidence in ourselves. We must also believe we are fashioned for greater things and that those things are within our reach. Properly embraced, self-confidence will help us further stretch our wings, and like the young eagle, we will soar to heights we never dreamed possible.

WHY MUST WE BELIEVE?

American philosopher William James (1842–1910) singled out one prominent cause for human failure: doubt. According to him, with faith in ourselves, we can breathe life into our goals. We must believe in ourselves regardless of the situation we are in. We should constantly remind ourselves that no matter how long or impossible our dreams may be, sooner or later, through the power of belief, we will achieve them. And even though the odds might seem to be against us, if we want to see that which we truly believe in come to fruition, we must be willing to do what others won't—thus defying the odds. Basically, if we convince ourselves that we will fail based on the fact that some already have, we are more likely to make that scenario a reality. Moreover, success and failure happen to those who believe in them. Choose wisely.

Acting with belief becomes a crucial factor for achieving success, be it in business, school, sports, or relationships. All these aspects are impacted by our belief systems. We often see that what we believe turns out to be the force that drives what we do. And what we do, in the long run, determines what we accomplish. When our beliefs are impregnable, we will perform highly and triumph over those whose beliefs are weak and not resilient. Tony Hsieh wrote, you've got to "Envision, create, and believe in your own universe, and the universe will form around you"[34]. Indeed, it is true that what we believe will either empower or limit us from becoming who we are meant to be. The power to believe lies in your choice.

Always remember:

With a strong belief
Comes relentless relief,
Taking you from shame
To an incomparable fame.

Now quit feeling sorry,
Rise up and achieve glory.
If needs be, accept mockery
So that you can celebrate victory.

Although many will come with insults,
Use that as an advantage to accumulate results.

Yes, you will need to engage in labour
For your fullness to be achieved in your favour.
Above all, do not see your failure as an acute disgrace.
Fairly, mentally, and wholesomely, accept it with grace.

---

[34] https://www.goodreads.com/author/quotes/3064249.Tony_Hsieh

We need to visualise what we intend to do. Sir Edmund Hillary said that with determination he ably hiked Mount Everest in 1953 after his previous failure in 1952[35]. This also applies to Sharon Wood, the first woman to hike the same world's highest mountain. We can clearly see that it is not the physical abilities the two had that enabled them to climb the mountain but their willingness and belief.

Ultradistance running champion Stu Mittleman, the American record holder for the 1,000-mile endurance run, is a physical mastery guru. In an interview, Mittleman was asked how he had geared up mentally for running the equivalent of nearly forty continuous marathons. Mittleman replied, "I never run 1,000 miles. I can't even conceive of running 1,000 miles. All I did was run one mile a thousand times"[36].

We might ask ourselves how he did it, right?

One thing I believe is that the great things, no matter how gigantic or complex, usually have small beginnings. If we have the zeal to accomplish something, we must believe we can. Often, when we doubt our abilities we shrink, sinking our future boat.

Every time we doubt our power and potential, we cultivate a fertile ground for doubt, which eventually leads to failure. What we feed our minds is important; it is crucial to feed it with possibilities.

THE SHARP MIND

The day started on a normal note, with birds singing joyfully and filled with happiness close to my bedroom window. So warm and promising was the weather on 20 August 2015. The fact that it was a beautiful Thursday morning could not be disputed; everything seemed to be in harmony with the creator himself.

My wife, Memory, and I were engaged in small talk. I affectionately call her Memo, for short. As we chatted, she was busy with a plastic bottle, trying to cut it[37]. I was mesmerised by the manner in which she proceeded—especially when she attempted to cut it with a pair of scissors.

"Ahhhh!" she exclaimed.

When I snapped, demanding to know what was going on, she quickly pointed out, "The pair of scissors has broken, honey", in an enchanting voice.

---

[35]   https://www.history.com/.amp/this-day-in-history/hillary-and-tenzing-reach-everest-summit.
[36]   https://ultrarunninghistory.com/hall-of-fame/hall-of-fame-stu-mittleman/
[37]   In Malawi empty plastic bottles can be cut to be used as a funnel (the top part), or a makeshift cup (bottom part)

Still bewildered as to what on earth she was doing, she brought out a razor blade and used it instead.

Seeing this as an opportunity to witness using a razor blade cutting through a bottle, I learnt with great interest from what had transpired and of its ability and contrasting difference, compared to a pair of scissors.

I was amazed by the extreme sharpness and efficiency of such a small thing as a razor blade. To some degree, I compared it to that of the human brain, at the same time taking into account the fact that one can be small in appearance yet sharp in mind and efficient in real life.

This is only achievable if one is trained for it. For such an awesome demonstration, I gave my wife a pat on the back. I believe we are all blessed with astonishing gifts and skills. It is through our minds that we can overcome limitations, transform all kinds of impossibilities into possibilities, or even perform miracles. We've got the whole world up in our minds, but to achieve all that is there, we must see beyond all that we can see.

In fact, the mind is the channel, the source, and the inspiration for unbelievable accomplishments. You need to be sharp minded to have clear-cut achievements.

THERE ARE NO LIMITATIONS

Far too many of us let our age, gender, race, upbringing, or economic status impede us from dreaming big. Often, we hold ourselves down, thinking we are either too old or too young to pursue our dreams. Owing to our mental barricade, we let our dreams pass without being fully exploited. Well, neither age nor gender is a barrier to success. How many successful people do you know of who have succeeded regardless of their age, gender, or background? A lot of them. Not so?

In his poem "Age's Not a Barrier",[38] Paul Sebastian elaborates on not using age as a limit to pursue our dreams.

> Age is but only a state of mind.
> Not to leave your dreams behind
> And let the little god in you die.
> In the waste land where quitters lie,

---

[38] https://www.poemhunter.com/poem/age-s-not-a-barrier/.

Wisdom and experience value more than gold.
Failure has no respect if you think you're old.
Success is for those who believe they can.
Age is not a barrier when you make your stand,
For success or failure is all in the state of mind.

Read the last sentence again: "For success or failure is all in the state of mind". Such eloquent and significant words, right? Indeed they are.

All the limitations around us are experienced within the scope of our own minds. We limit ourselves by our own thinking, not our age. There is nothing wrong with our age; we are not too young or too old, we are just fine. Most of the time people use age or gender as an excuse not to achieve their goals. For example, just because one is a lady does not limit her from getting a managerial role that is normally managed by men. Likewise, being a lady does not mean you can never own a successful enterprise. No! Those are just limitations perceived by small-minded people.

As far as success is concerned, there is nothing like that. If being a lady was a limitation to achieving dreams, JK Rowling wouldn't have become a successful author and philanthropist. She has won numerous accolades and sold more than five hundred million copies of the Harry Potter series, which have been translated into at least seventy languages, generating a global media franchise including movies and video games. Is she not a lady? She certainly is. Then what is your excuse?

Contemplating the lives of highly successful people, you will notice that behind their greatness is one common thing: they did not allow anything to determine their destiny. Most believed profusely in their potential and ability to succeed.

For instance, Colonel Harland Sanders, an American entrepreneur who began selling fried chicken from his roadside restaurant, was older than sixty when he made it big with Kentucky Fried Chicken (KFC). He was at an age when most people dream of retiring, yet Sanders was at that age busy building his global empire. Sanders did not use his age as a barrier; instead, he used it as fuel to drive his passion towards the success of his dream.

On the other hand, Mark Zuckerberg, an internet entrepreneur and founder of Facebook became the world's youngest billionaire at age twenty-three. Zuckerberg became a huge success at a young age. Did he use his age as a barrier? No! For Zuckerberg, his age has proven to be an advantage, in case you were wondering if there was an age to start pursuing your dreams. There isn't. Evidently, there is no specific age to start chasing your personal dreams—it is now or never.

No age is the wrong age. Old age does not mean your time to dream big has elapsed, nor that young age is a handicap for an early start towards the journey of your success. Never let age dictate what you can and cannot do. Both Zuckerberg and Sanders worked consistently towards their personal goals regardless of their age. Do you still think age is a barrier to success?

To achieve our dreams and succeed, we should not allow ourselves to be held down by our circumstances or the limitations in our environment. We should not be dragged down by insecurities (fears and doubts in our minds) but rather should be influenced by the dreams in our hearts. We must fuel ourselves with belief and a positive mindset.

Lack of belief will neither get you a star on America's Hollywood Walk of Fame nor a British Victoria Cross. To reach for the stars, one must dream big and kick self-doubt in the behind.

Lack of belief is one of the single most destructive impediments to the achievement of a goal or the realisation of any dream.

6

HOW TO
SUCCEED IN LIFE

Success is no accident. It is hard work, perseverance, learning, studying,
sacrifice and most of all, love of what you are doing or learning to do.
—Edson Arantes do Nascimento, Brazilian Professional Footballer

First and foremost, success is a mind game. It is nothing but a set of invisible inner beliefs (IIBs) that we always carry with us. We must be aware that we have at our disposal all that we need in order to become all we are destined to be. Also, be advised that the limitations we experience each day are the result of limited thinking and limited belief. To succeed, we must get rid of all limiting beliefs.

What is success to you? To me, success refers to all things that make us feel happy and comfortable within our environment, including personal achievements. Everyone wants to succeed and not be plagued with an inferiority complex. Well then, if our desire is to live a successful life, we must start planning for it, keeping in mind that success is not served on a silver platter, nor does it fall from heaven like manna but follows discipline and hard work.

SETTING UP GOALS THAT COULD LEAD TO SUCCESS

Structuring clear goals, coupled with a comprehensive plan of action to accomplish those goals is necessary to achieve success. Without goals, we cannot measure our success. If we do not have goals, we can easily be swayed and eventually lose focus. Do not go through life without focus or not knowing your purpose. Author Robert Byrne said, "The purpose of life is to live a life of purpose". We should set our goals and plans realistically and then put them down in black and white so we can easily follow them.

WHAT ARE GOALS?

Goals are the intended results of our plans. Our goals can only be reached through plans we must believe in and vigorously act upon with passion. To reach our goals, we should set high standards. Never settle for less. Always aim high. Achieving any goal can be challenging and often requires perseverance. If we shoot too low, we are less likely to experience success. Setting high standards makes every day worth looking forward to.

As oxygen is important to human life, goals are an essential part of the life of your dreams. It does not matter how vivid your dreams are; without goals, your dreams will not be manifested into reality. Goals are like a handy map aiding you to navigate the terrain of your dreams. They are a benchmark that enable you to pursue your dreams with purpose.

One exciting and challenging point in my life was during our Royal Marines commando training course in Lympstone, England, when we were tested on our prowess to navigate. The test involved individually navigating for ten kilometres from one checkpoint to another within a specified period of two hours. It was such an unforgettable moment that sent shivers down my spine. Considering that the test would be conducted in one of the roughest areas ever imagined, I prepared my mind for the worst-case scenario. For a moment, I held my breath and said, "What? Me?" But I gathered courage and told myself I would do it. After all, I had accepted the challenge to join the military and excel at every test and stage of training.

The weather was chilly, the night pitch-black; I could hardly see anything. Tactically, we were apprised to not use the white light on our head torches. This not only prolonged my night but made the terrain treacherous. I nearly died that night, and I have never revealed this to anyone before.

Based on the route card, I was doing perfectly well on the test, until I got to the last checkpoint while returning to base. I had been to all three allocated checkpoints in good time, and it was time to start heading back. This was when the unexpected happened. Being so dark and dangerous, I had to make sure I did not incur any injuries, as this could have resulted in failing the course.

But gosh! There I was out in the cold and dark, heading back to base (at an approximate distance of one kilometre) when I got lost. I glanced at my map to see where I was. I decided I could take a short turn along the way, which was when the shit hit the fan, as they say. I knew something was wrong, but I was yet to find out. Alas! There I was, caught in a bog and sinking like a stone with my full kit.

In no time I had sunk all the way to my chest. All my struggling at this point was futile because both my hands and legs were stuck. All alone, in absolute darkness, I was deeply despondent. As this was an Individual exercise and I was well within the allocated time, It quickly occurred to me that no one was coming to my rescue—no Calvary, no hand to pull me out. My survival was my responsibility. I had to save myself.

At this moment, time was not on my side, yet I had two things on my mind: a test to pass and my precious life to save. It was either one of them or none. After a few minutes in solitude, I managed to gather the strength to reach out for my rifle, which by then was stuck in the mud by my righthand side. I tugged it off and expeditiously used it to propel myself out, with only one thing in mind: *I cannot die today*. Sounds simple, right? Not at all. It was a struggle between life and death.

Even though it took me about thirty minutes to finally free myself, I did not give in to defeat. Determined not to be beaten, I fought my way out until I managed to grab some grass that was by the side. Hallelujah! The mission was accomplished. Covered in mud, I ran the remaining four hundred meters to base.

My kit was now heavy from the mud, I was exhausted and in terrible pain, but I kept running until I reached the base three minutes over the required time. On that night, no one knew I had fought the angel of death beneath the dungeon.

At this stage, I felt inclined to believe that, just like navigation, life is sometimes similar to finding a bearing on a map. At some point, even with our goals intact, we find ourselves off course. But when such occasions transpire, all we've got to do is quickly *stop*! Check the map and adjust accordingly (re-strategise). If need be, get a new bearing (changing our goals), and set off in a different direction. Truly, if I had clearly checked the terrain on the map before setting off on the grid references given, I wouldn't have found myself in that bog.

In summary, we are all going to be off-track at some point; such is life. Not giving in to defeat has been my attitude, and it has stood me in great stead when faced with setbacks. This was ingrained in me from the days when I was a barefoot kid wandering the streets.

We should consider the words of Confucius, who said, "When it is obvious that the goals cannot be reached, don't adjust the goals, adjust the action steps"[39]. When it comes to goal setting, not all will manifest as planned. As part of a transformation process, we must cultivate a strong will to be flexible and adapt to new changes. Being flexible will help us fully evolve and bring about tremendous changes in our lives.

The legendary twentieth-century martial artist Bruce Lee wrote the same about goals. According to his teachings, he said, "A goal is not always meant to be reached. It often serves simply as something to aim at"[40]. When pursuing goals, we must remember to keep them as SMART (specific measurable attainable realistic time) as possible. SMART is a method that has been adopted by many, including psychologists, when it comes to goal setting.

SPECIFICS

Your goals need to be well-defined and crystal clear. Time and again, before pursuing any goal, ask yourself, "What do I want to achieve?" "How will I achieve it?" "When will I achieve it?" As they say, failing to plan is planning to fail. You will not achieve anything if you don't plan accordingly.

---

[39] https://philosiblog.com/2011/09/27/when-it-is-obvious-that-the-goals-cannot-be-reached-don't--adjust-the-goals-adjust-the-action-steps/ .

[40] Bruce Lee, *Tao of Jeet Kun Do* (Black Belt Books, 2011)

MEASURABLE RESULTS

Scrutinise your goals to align with the measure of your success. Confucius said, "The man who moves a mountain begins by carrying away small stones".

To achieve bigger goals, start by taking action on the smaller ones. For instance, if your goal is to run a marathon, start by running a mile every day to prepare yourself mentally and physically. The small achievements measure your success towards your goal.

ATTAINABLE RESULTS

Plan your goals in such a way that they are attainable and not impossible to achieve. The reason many people fail is because the goals are vague. Remember, Confucius warned us: "A person who chases two rabbits catches neither".

Pursuing a lot of goals at the same time often leads to failure. So when setting your goals, make sure to focus and follow through on each goal.

REALISTIC GOALS

Your goals need to be real, not indefinite. They should be relevantly set and tailored according to your final product, which is the purpose of your life. From a practicality standpoint, goals that are ground breaking and life changing are perceived as achievable.

BOUND BY TIME

Time becomes crucial when it comes to goal setting. I have learnt that "A goal without a timeline is just a dream"[41], according to Croatian-Canadian businessman, investor, and television personality Robert Herjavec. It is important to maintain a deadline aligned with your goals. Apparently, goals that are not timely managed or date oriented manifest into mediocre dreams.

CLASSIFICATION OF GOALS

Goals can be classified into three timelines, as explained in the following:

- **Short Term**

  These goals are often attained within a short period of time. Such goals are often achieved within one to two years.

---

[41] https://www.linkedin.com/pulse/goals-without-timelines-just-dreams-adam-ashcroft?trk=public_profile_article_view

- **Medium Term**

  These goals are achievable within a moderately longer period, usually between four and five years.

- **Long Term**

  These goals are achieved after many years—often five or more. Sometimes the period might go as far as a decade or more.

All three goals are important, but in all fairness, we must be focused to attain the best results since the duration each one takes is not a serious matter on its own. There is common thinking that setting up goals is an eventual determinant of what can be achieved. There is more to it than that, though. We must understand that goals alone are not enough.

Many successful people made plans to reach their current status. Success is an intentional component that requires a strong will and a vivid plan. When we plan our lives, God guides us to better results. He takes us to appropriate places at the right time.

We may ask ourselves if success is the source of happiness. In my experience, success does not breed happiness, but rather, happiness yields success. This might sound unusual, but you might agree that there are many people who are successful yet are unhappy.

What is your vision for the future? How do you see your life to be in the next five, ten, fifteen, or even twenty years? And if you are able to visualise your future, have you got your goals aligned?

You will never achieve your goals until you identify what they really are. Do you know what you want and how to get it? Have you put your goals in writing so you can check on them? Once you put your goals on paper, you will see that they become easy to access, follow through, and achieve.

The idea of leaving behind all I had achieved in Malawi, going into the diaspora, and starting again from scratch was inconceivable and beyond belief. This was to be a daunting task and a crucial moment that needed considerable thought and analysis.

It was not a decision that would be made hastily, and upon looking back and considering all the hard work and sweetness of pleasure from the little success I had tasted, I felt insecure and hesitant for a moment.

As a result of being comfortable and satisfied with my status, it took me time to finally decide on what I wanted to do next. Finally, after some solitary time and meditation, I accepted my fate with a positive attitude and courage, thereby following what had transpired. I then learnt there is no fear greater than that of leaving your comfort zone to start all over again, mostly into an environment where nobody knows you.

We will find ourselves in tight spots and difficult circumstances that will force us to make decisions with minimal or no consideration. To that end, when filled with emotions of fear, doubt, and low self-esteem, we need to shake off negativity and redirect our focus towards the end goal, which is our vision.

Instead of acting on our doubts and fears, we should be emotionally content and contemplate possibilities that might arise if we took the initiative to pursue our dreams. Most of the time, people who don't have the courage to say no to self-doubt and fear languish in mediocrity. They remain on the same level and never achieve anything of significance. In order to achieve success, you should never be afraid to become uncommon.

In his book *The Success Principles*, Jack Canfield said, "Only those who dare to fail greatly can achieve greatly"[42]. If we want to achieve great things, we must allow ourselves to fail and learn from our failures. We should embrace our ups and downs because that will give us a chance to experience life's greatest lessons. Furthermore, when we fail, we will understand what works well and what doesn't.

As explained previously, failure offers us many valuable lessons, which in the end will assist us with the response to it. This is to say it will either make us or break us. But before doing all this, we must have a positive mindset to believe we have what it takes to succeed.

Being delivered from the fangs of poverty in Malawi has taught me valuable lessons, including the realisation of my ability to survive under any circumstances. The truth is, if you can make it out from the streets of Malawi, you can make it anywhere. All the lessons I learnt when I was a 'hopeless ghetto child' have paid generously.

Through overcoming challenges, I've come to learn that life's greatest lessons can sometimes be understood best by jumping into the deep end. Perhaps every one of us will come across this moment, and when your turn comes, embrace it with courage, and confidently jump. In the deep end is where all your insecurities reside, and if you are afraid to take risks, you will never realise the potential that is already within you.

---

[42] Jack Canfield, *The Success Principles (HarperNonFiction, 2005)*

With regards to experience, the only thing that is standing between most people and their dreams is themselves. For that reason, if you are willing to get to the other (better) side of life, where all the heavenly glory dwells, all you need to do is take a leap of faith and risk everything.

For the past ten years I was blind to change and had settled into my comfort zone. All I needed to do and become was right in front of me, yet I could not perceive it. Clearly, if you are in your comfort zone and operating under the influence of fear and doubt, your success will be limited and won't be fully and abundantly manifested in your life.

LEADING AN INSPIRATIONAL LIFE

Strategic planning and belief are prerequisites to achieving our goals. There is no other route to success than understanding the secret of enthusiasm. All our dreams can come to pass if we believe and have the courage to pursue them. When times are tough, we must find inspiration to help us cling to things we excel at.

We can be inspired by listening to music, by praying, or by reading motivational books. Through doing such things we can be encouraged to keep going when the going gets tough. Dwelling on or obsessing over the problems we face does nothing to help the situation; instead, we should interact with people who can motivate us. Interacting with people can help us get new ideas through their experiences.

We should seek as much inspiration as possible to keep us on track; additionally, we should not doubt our capabilities. Doubt hinders our abilities and we fail to achieve anything tangible. We should have confidence in our abilities and be vigilant to follow through.

Denis Waitley, in his book *The New Psychology of Winning*, says, "The winners in life think constantly in terms of I can, I will, and I am. Losers, on the other hand, concentrate their waking thoughts on what they should have or would have done, or what they can't do"[43]. Essentially, if we believe we can do something, that becomes the foundation of our victory. But if we think on the contrary, we have already been defeated no matter how hard we try.

If we live expectant lives, we end up getting what we have been anticipating. That is to say, if we expect the best, we are prone to get it, but if we anticipate the worst, we shall get it as well. Every person will at some point be faced with challenges that would discourage him or her in one way or another, but that should not limit us or make us look down upon ourselves.

---

43   Denis Waitley, *The Psychology of Winning (Warner Books, 1989)*

ASKING FOR ASSISTANCE

Turbulence should expose us to seeking opportunities that can foster our determination to live according to our set values and goals. We should take barricades as stepping stones towards building the type of lives we want. It's normal to feel lonely and rejected when tough times emerge. However, we should also realise that there are people who can lend an ear or a helping hand, but all we must do is ask for their help. Many people have survived hectic moments and points of almost quitting, but with assistance from others, they sailed through. We all need supportive friends on whom we can lean for help or support. Generally, there is little one can achieve with a single hand, but with support from others, much can be done.

Doing things with others brings contentment. Besides that, people who tackle problems alone are usually anxious and get themselves into trouble or fail to register remarkable results.

Mother Teresa once said, "I can do things you cannot, you can do things I cannot; together we can do great things". Similarly, others could do what she might not be able to do.

Motivation, just like it sounds, is a fire burning within our inner selves. It is an inner state that seeks to direct us towards achieving our goals. If someone tries to motivate us, chances are high that we can prevail, but only if we take the motivation seriously. We should neither be boastful nor feel too embarrassed when asking for assistance.

We should try as much as possible to express ourselves in such a way that we can really induce assistance. In the sea of humanity, no person is an island. That's why we need each other. We should also ask God to bring us the right people.

The great Chinese philosopher Confucius said, "It is difficult to ascend to the sky, but it is even more so to seek the help of others. A wise man does not rely on others, nor does he place all his hopes upon them"[44]. When seeking assistance, we should not expect too much from others; otherwise, we might get disappointed if they give us the cold shoulder.

Success is a two-way street. Take some time to network with people who are in the same field as you. Be more than willing to learn under those who know more than you do. Never be too proud or afraid to learn, and humble yourself so you can be assisted by those who know. No one can teach you more than someone who has already been there. As opposed to common knowledge, many people feel it is a weakness to admit that they don't know

---

[44]   https://books-that-can-change-your-life.net/quotes-from-confucius/

something, well, admitting that one does not know something depicts strength and it is an opportunity to grow and learn.

According to the *Tao Te Ching*[45], Laozi is saying

> Those who know they do not know gain wisdom, Those who pretend they know remain ignorant. Those who acknowledge their weakness become strong. Those who flaunt their power will lose it. Wisdom and power follow truth above all, for truth is the way of the Tao.

Don't be afraid to ask for the help you need in order to live the life you deserve. You should seek assistance often. Ask for help when you must, but remember, no one is reading your mind to see if you need help.

To that end, do not make assumptions thinking someone will come to your aid and save you from drowning in despair.

You must ask for help to be helped. In the scriptures, it's well said that "Ask, and it will be given to you; seek, and you will find; knock, and it will be opened to you"[46].

Are you searching for greener pastures? Are you knocking and opening new doors to welcome new opportunities? In general, are you asking for what you want in life? You will never achieve anything if you don't ask.

Also, be aware that whilst asking for help, people might not be willing to offer it. Therefore, do not take their *no* to be your final say. If you get *no* as an answer, remember that *no* means you should move on to your next opportunity. Keep asking, believing, and knocking until you get the help you need.

FORGET ABOUT MAKING MISTAKES

We have all made mistakes at some point. Making a mistake is not the same as failing. You can make thousands of mistakes, but that does not characterise you as a failure. There is a huge difference between them. Have you not seen people who, regardless of their mistakes, still succeed?

---

[45]   Lao Tzu, *Tao Te Ching (Capstone, 2012).*
[46]   Matthew 7:7 New King James Version

Failure comes as a result of the wrong action, whereas a mistake is usually the wrong action. This is to say, when you make a mistake, you can learn from and fix it, whereas you can only learn from a failure.

After all, it is not a bad thing to make mistakes, but if we don't use our mistakes as lessons, we will absolutely fail, never achieving anything remarkable. Alexander Pope said to err is human. Clearly we do not have to feel sorry for ourselves over mistakes made.

Mistakes happen for a reason; they could be great opportunities in disguise, or they might be there to offer lessons.

As a matter of course, mistakes will always be there since they are part of it and sometimes inevitable. The most important thing we should bear in mind is not accepting our previous mistakes to control our present situation or define our destiny. More importantly, we should never be tempted to regret our previous mistakes; instead, we should forge ahead with extra energy. Dwelling on our mistakes with self-condemnation and shame only prolongs the pain.

We should have time to reflect on our previous failures for the purposes of learning to prevent their recurrence. We must learn to evaluate areas we performed well in and those where we performed poorly so we are able to understand our failures as well as our successes. Evaluation often helps us make better decisions. Mistakes are painful, but after correcting them they breed often successful experiences. It is impossible to circumvent mistakes and pitfalls, so do not be afraid of failure. When you fail or hit rock bottom, always try to look on the bright side of life because moaning over failure will get you nowhere.

Most of the time we find it is easy to do what we are used to doing and staying within the confines of least resistance. But if we want to make significant progress in our lives, we need to break free from what is holding us back—our fear of failure or making mistakes. Inasmuch as we cannot win a ball game by always playing defence, we will never succeed by always choosing the easy way out. This means that by following the road with less resistance, the one with no risks, mistakes, and challenges, we will not amount to anything or achieve anything of consequence.

UNDERSTANDING YOUR STEPPING STONES

Barricades are obstacles we face while on the journey of attaining success, but they are also regarded as building blocks of life. Such things will always be there, but we should not consent to them to define what we handle or how we might handle similar situations in the future. Thinking big or having talent does not necessarily mean we are free from challenges. We shall always have them, but the way we choose to handle them will determine our destiny.

It is up to us as individuals to decide whether to treat roadblocks as barriers or as a step towards moving forward. If we choose to look at problems as barriers, we will have trouble proceeding. But if we look at them as stepping stones, we can progress in our endeavours. All people who have prevailed also faced challenges at one point in their lives, but they chose to carry on regardless of the challenges. For me, bone-crushing poverty was a huge stumbling block.

We often need to realise that every problem we encounter can give us strength and prepare us for the next challenge. Brazilian lyricist and novelist Paulo Coelho de Souza said, "An arrow can only be shot by pulling it backward. So when life is dragging you back with difficulties, it means it's going to launch you into something great. So just focus and keep aiming".[47]

On the path to discover the secret to success, one thing remains clear: every obstacle we face defines who we are and gives us confidence. Success is biased as it only goes to people who do things differently. We should, therefore, have the mindset that should accept the dynamic nature of life.

Influential figures we know today, never allowed difficulties to bar them from reaching their goals. They embraced change and chose not to succumb to mediocrity and poverty.

Hellene Schucman and William Thetford once wrote that "Every situation that is handled and looked at from a positive perspective becomes an opportunity"[48]. We can all become whatever we want, but only if we learn to understand our stepping stones and never let barricades define us. However, if we are afraid to learn and use our stepping stones as fuel and motivation, we will crumble at any challenge we encounter.

On the other hand, if we don't take some risks and do things that scare us, we will never really understand who we truly are. We often learn the most about ourselves when we walk openly into challenges. This is because by learning about ourselves, we can overcome, survive, and challenge any obstacle in front of us, thus emerging stronger, more experienced, and wise.

---

[47] https://www.quotespedia.org/authors/p/paulo-coelho/an-arrow-can-only-be-shot-by-pulling-it-backward-so-when-life-is-dragging-you-back-with-difficulties-it-means-that-its-going-to-launch-you-into-something-great-so-just-focus-and-keep-aiming-p/.

[48] https://www.azquotes.com/quote/520108

By all means, while being honest and realistic, the more challenges we face, the stronger and more confident we will become. Using this philosophy, we should all strive to use our challenges, setbacks, and roadblocks as stepping stones. And despite being afraid and in doubt, we must be willing to push ourselves forward, because

Hard work never lies.
Your dream never dies.
Only if you become fearless
Will your life become limitless.[49]

DON'T REST IN YOUR COMFORT ZONE

One fine Wednesday afternoon I was heading home from giving private martial arts lessons to some of my students. I took a familiar route, one that passed a major hospital, Bwaila Hospital.

As I advanced past the hospital gate. I saw a visually impaired man who appeared to be in his early forties playing the guitar. His also visually impaired wife (I assumed she was his wife), who looked to be in her mid-thirties, was playing a small drum. With them on the side was presumably their child, who seemed to be about a year old. The child was unmindfully playing with dirt.

Being a common sight in the township, I initially did not give the scene much thought. But as I drew closer, I heard a song from the man's direction. His singing was in perfect harmony with his guitar.

His voice was exceptional. The closer I got, the more absorbed I became in the lyrics and the deep meaning they carried, and something stirred within me.

The song was sung in vernacular, and if memory serves, it went, "*Khwangwala wamantha anafa ndi ukalamba*", which literally translates to, "A fearful, cowardly crow dies of old age". One common translation of this proverb is that if you are afraid of action, of coming out of your comfort zone, you will die of old age. You will age quickly.

I immediately stopped because I found the meaning profound. I understood that to attain our hearts' desires, we must be willing to take risks without having any fear because fear restrains us from achieving success. If we let fear control us from trying new things, then premature "death by old age" will be the only result. At any given time, we must be

---

49   Adapted from https://notalonenow.com/hard-work-never-lies-ft-jones-2-0-lyrics-fearless-motivation/

willing to give up all that we have in order to become all that we can be. If we do that, if we are willing to leave our comfort zone and bravely keep striving, we can reach heights we thought were beyond us. We can go further than those who possess greater capabilities than ourselves.

A comfort zone is when we are content with our situations or environment. For us to achieve great things, we should not be satisfied with our current status quo; we must be willing to take risks to move from a better situation to the best one. Fear is a venom that restrains us from achieving success, so it should not be given room in our lives.

We must be willing to give up all we have to reach our destination. If we are willing to leave our comfort zones and bravely strive to achieve something, we can finally reach immeasurable heights, even beyond those we imagined.

According to Leonardo da Vinci, "It had long since come to my attention that people of accomplishment rarely sat back and let things happen to them. They went out and happened to things".[50]

To achieve massive and meaningful success, we must get out of our comfort zones. We can't depend on them and expect to reach our optimum potential. Biblical scriptures tell us about how Simon Peter one time admired how his master was walking on water; the first step he took was to get out of the boat. Similarly, we have so much ability in us that can be realised only if we confidently rise.

You will fail if you stay in your comfort zone. Steve Harvey said, "Success is not a comfortable procedure. It is a very uncomfortable thing, so you need to get comfortable being uncomfortable"[51]. Often, when you push yourself beyond your limits and comfort, you discover inner reserves you never thought existed. Here is a poem called "Comfort Zone"; author unknown.

> I used to have a comfort zone where I knew I couldn't fail.
> The same four walls of busywork were really more like jail.
> I longed so much to do the things I'd never done before,
> But I stayed inside my comfort zone and paced the same old floor.

We should get into the habit of walking away from our comfort zones. We should step further away from the confines of the comfort zone that limits us to fully evolve as

---

50   https://www.ncbi.nlm.nih.gov/pmc/articles/PMC2681055/#:~:text=Leonardo%20da%20Vinci%3A%20%E2%80%9CIt%20had,out%20and%20happened%20to%20things.%E2%80%9D.

51   Steve Harvey, *Act Like a Success (Amistad, 2015)*

complete and limitless beings. The more we do this, the better we will learn, experience, and understand what life must furnish us with. Finally, we will be able to defy the odds against us. And guess what will happen next? We will achieve resounding success.

PROBLEMS ASSOCIATED WITH A COMFORT ZONE

- **It Stunts Growth**

Lingering in our comfort zone will keep us at ease and less productive. Our lives become more fulfilling and meaningful when we learn and grow. But when we are stuck in our safety nets, our growth is compressed and limited. Being in a comfort zone is risky to our success. Every day we are presented with opportunities to change our lives, but that can never happen if we are relaxed and cosy in our comforts. Relaxation in our comfort zone will prevent our dreams from coming to their full realisation.

- **It Chokes Potential**

Sometimes the reason so many of us are not where we want to be is that we are confined to our comfort zones. However, if we step out, we will begin to see our horizon expanding above and beyond what we've always perceived. In the long run, this will lead to higher perspectives, perhaps bringing about newfound opportunities. Bruce Lee said "People who love life don't waste time".

He added that every man's greatest capital asset is his unexpired years of productivity[52]. Every minute of a person's life should be spent purposefully. Don't waste time by wasting time; invest your time wisely.

Nevertheless, we should at no point settle down in our comfort zone and accept mediocrity or allow poverty to have a final say. We were not created to be poor or average achievers. Therefore, no matter what we might face or how difficult our situations might appear, we must press hard and keep reminding ourselves that our circumstances can improve. We should break out of our comfort zones.

THERE ARE NO EXCUSES

It was at noon on 25 August, the year was 2015, I was making my way past Bwaila Hospital, the usual route. This time I was heading back home from work after having taken lunch at a restaurant nearby. I noticed a couple with a child and visible at this moment were the seeds of love, happiness, and compassion planted around them.

---

[52]   Bruce Lee, *Tao of Jeet Kun Do (Black Belt Books, 2011)*

It was the visually impaired couple I had met the other day, seated at the usual place under the scorching sun that could have made most uncomfortable with its sweltering heat. The man sat with a smile, his son on his lap, but this time his favourite instrument was by his side. I watched him with keen interest and was bewildered by what I saw.

The man was changing his son's soiled nappies. Deep inside me, I thought, *Is this really happening?* It was the first time in my life seeing a person with visual impairment able to do that and with love, care, and concern. Despite being at a distance, I was convinced by the movement of his lips that he might have been singing to the baby, just to keep him happy.

This man not only executed the task excellently but fulfilled it without an excuse. It was well apparent to me that his perfection might have come a long way from defying the use of his status as an excuse, especially to avoid certain tasks.

Good Samaritans could have come to his aid, had he asked for help using his disability as an excuse. But this great man opted to apply his sense of commitment, responsibility, and independence very well, regardless of help, even from his own wife, who was seated by his side.

From this experience I discovered that there are no disabilities, except those we impose on ourselves. Many people have been programmed with an excuses mentality, and there is not a single thing that they do without having an excuse.

Taking heed of the fact that an excuse is a foundation upon which one builds a house of failure, it brings us back to awareness that each time we make an excuse, we allow failure to take hold. When we use excuses, we block our progress and waste time and energy.

There are many times that we are going to fall, but we should stop making excuses. We need to learn to accept blame or responsibility in order to improve ourselves. One thing for sure is that failures are experts at making excuses. It's been said that an excuse is a thin skin of falsehood stretched tightly over a bald-faced lie.

Unlike the visually impaired man, so many people have acquired the wrong mindset and go by the status quo that says success is a matter of luck. But that only comes out of the mouth of people who have failed, people who don't want to make a difference in life, or people who only accept mediocrity and succumb to poverty.

In the book of Proverbs, it's written, "All hard work brings a profit, but mere talk leads only to poverty"[53]. Live a no-excuses life and make progress towards accomplishing great levels.

SEEKING THE RIGHT COMPANIONS

The path to prosperity can be both funny and tricky, sometimes leading people to misery. But what it mostly requires is to be selective with the kind of people we associate with. To live a successful and fruitful life, we need to choose the type of environment that can benefit us. This applies to our interactions with people who can impact our lives both positively and negatively.

When associating with others, choose carefully who you surround yourself with. Plato said, "People are like dirt. They can either nourish you and help you grow as a person, or they can stunt your growth and make you wilt and die".[54]Who is in your circle? Are they adding any value to your life? If yes, happy days! But if not, what are you doing about it?

Time and again we neglect the impact other people might have on our lives. Whether it is in sports, business, and relationships, we will somehow be affected consciously or subconsciously by others. To be honest, there is an infinite power that emanates from relationships. Beyond scepticism, this points directly to our day-to-day associations with others, who in the long run will either help us to succeed or cause us to flounder.

Be advised, before building a relationship of any kind with anyone, it is imperative to first consider how that relationship could be of great help to you and the achievement of your dreams. As a glass of water, a relationship can be perceived as a means to an end, which can either quench your thirst and nourish your body for intellectual growth. Or it can choke your potential and limit your success. It all depends on the decisions you make.

If a relationship that you seek or have does not add value or bring you any closer to the meaning and purpose of your life, that relationship should be considered meaningless and not worth pursuing. It is wise to do yourself a favour and walk away from it.

A recent study by psychologists shows that different aspects of life can be enriched through meaningful relationships[55]. This is to say the more we find meaning and understand how relationships operate, the more we can learn, grow, and benefit from them. Motivational speaker Jim Rohn once said, "You are the average of the five people you spend the most

---

[53] *Proverbs 14:23 New International Version*
[54] https://www.brainyquote.com/quotes/plato_392892#:~:text=Plato%20Quotes&text=Please%20enable%20 Javascript,People%20are%20like%20dirt.,make%20you%20wilt%20and%20die.
[55] https://www.keithmillercounseling.com/indivudual-therapy-for-relationships/

time with".[56] This only concludes that the right circle of influence will raise your bar, thereby helping you succeed at a higher level.

If we live in an environment with people of negative attitudes towards things, low self-esteem, and a decayed mindset, we cannot prevail. It's deadly to maintain such friendships, so don't feel worried about terminating any regressive friendships since they are good for nothing other than shattering our dreams and retarding our development.

Ostensibly, our environment influences what we are, so strive to be in a positive environment that can help you to nurture growth or support your dreams and career.

It has been written, " But others fell on good ground and yielded a crop: some a hundredfold, some sixty, some thirty"[57]. Similarly, great ideas and talents without channelling them properly to the right people will amount to nothing. Believe it or not, your network equals your net worth. Take the time to network with people who are in the same field as you.

Generally speaking, the quality of our lives is directly connected to the quality of our relationships with the people in our lives.

Plutarch said, "[I]f you live with a lame man, you will learn to limp".[58] Often, if you surround yourself with great people, chances are that sooner or later you will also become great. In other words, surround yourself with people who will encourage you to be all that you can become. All things considered, desperate times call for desperate measures.

The adage, "There is a purpose for everyone you meet", is so accurate when it comes to seeking the right companions. People will come into our lives for various reasons, some bad, some good. Some will either come to teach us or destroy us, to bring the best out of us or even drain us.

The question is, how are we welcoming people into our circle? Are we allowing them to dictate our future? (Which they shouldn't.) Or are we cautiously analysing who we allow in? If the people in your circle tend to threaten your peace of mind, your self-respect, your values, morals, and self-worth, it is imperative to find the exit and see yourself out peacefully.

---

[56] https://personalexcellence.co/blog/average-of-5-people/.
[57] Matthew 13:8 New King James Version
[58] https://quotefancy.com/quote/889449/Plutarch-It-is-a-true-proverb-that-if-you-live-with-a-lame-man-you-will-learn-to-limp.

While seeking the right companionship from others, you must be aware of desperate people. These are the kind of people who will come to you with the right thing for the wrong reasons. They will walk along your path just to make sure they witness you fail to accomplish your dreams. Rumour has it that not everyone who claps for you is for you. Others do that to warm their hands to slap you.

7

REASONS PEOPLE
GIVE UP

All life demands struggle. Those who have everything given to them become lazy, selfish, and insensitive to the real values of life. The very striving and hard work that we so constantly try to avoid is the major building block in the person we are today.
—Albert Einstein

Following a series of disappointments, people sometimes give up. In those moments, we need a little patience, faith, positive thinking, and strength to move on. Faith gives us hope and encouragement to go the extra mile when things go in the opposite direction. Whenever we face hurdles we should not give up; rather, we should stand up against the challenge(s) and do something.

In *The Power of Positive Thinking*, Norman Vincent Peale wrote, "People are not defeated because they are unable to do things but because they lack willpower, they do not wholeheartedly expect to succeed"[59]. To succeed, as well as overcome our challenges, we must believe we will do so. The will to succeed brings us one step closer to success.

THE FEAR OF FAILING

Oftentimes, most people give up just when they are about to make a breakthrough or achieve greatness. They quit right at success's one-yard line at the last minute of the game, just one yard from a winning touchdown.

Famed American cognitive-behavioural therapist Albert Ellis said, "The best years of your life are the ones in which you decide your problems are your own. You do not blame them on your mother, the ecology, or the president. You realise that you control your own destiny".[60]

One of the main reasons many people fail to succeed is that they have a *monkey mind*, which, according to Wikipedia, is "a Buddhist term meaning unsettled; restless; capricious; whimsical; fanciful; inconstant; confused; indecisive; and uncontrollable"[61]—in other words, a mind that jumps from one branch of life to another without being decisive.

To achieve greatness, you need clear-cut goals and then find possible ways of getting there. But if you can't made up your mind, you will be nowhere. Remember, as Zig Ziglar said, "If you aim at nothing, you'll hit it every time".[62] Decide what you want to do and fearlessly go for it.

---

[59]   Norman Vincent Peale, *The Power of Positive Thinking* (Cedar Books / vermilion, 1990)

[60]   https://www.psychologytoday.com/us/blog/how-do-life/201608/albert-ellis-quote#:~:text=The%20famed%20cognitive%2Dbehavioral%20therapist,you%20control%20your%20own%20destiny.%22.

[61]   https://en.wikipedia.org/wiki/Monkey_mind#:~:text=Monkey%20mind%20or%20mind%20monkey,confused%3B%20indecisive%3B%20uncontrollable%22.

[62]   https://www.brainyquote.com/quotes/zig_ziglar_617761

Fear

Unseen and unscathed
Emanates the force from within.
Deeply rooted and shapeless,
Inside the heart it is found.
Controlled and embraced,
Magnificently it is overcome.

Unnoticed and uncontrolled,
So bad the outcome is produced.
Without visibility of form,
It is perceived by the physicality of man's troubled nature.

Existing in one's eyes,
Seen from the body's vibration,
Felt from the racing heartbeat,
Its manifestation is nakedly said in four letters.

Arising from an unpleasant emotion
Comes with it thoughts of worry.
Born or not born with it,
Still gets room inside everyone.
Like a fog mercilessly obscuring your vision,
It causes heartbreaks and mouths agape.

As I've discovered, the fear of stepping into the unknown inhibits self-realisation as well as growth. This became my experience in basic training when I signed up for the commando course, the longest and toughest infantry training in the world. It scares a magnitude of people. Some things can be avoided, but not when you tread on the path of becoming a commando. Unlike many of my friends I went into basic training with, I was amongst the few who had the audacity and willingness to endure the hardships and difficulty of this formidable training.

Going through the Royal Marines commando training in Lympstone, England, was an absolutely tough and challenging experience. The path taught me numerous valuable lessons and elevated me to a level I never thought feasible. In a nutshell, Lympstone gave no room for inconsistency and futile mistakes; each of us was held accountable for conduct that was only expected to be of the highest standard.

The instructors, being well experienced and on top of their game, paid close attention to detail. A single act of nuisance by an individual meant everyone got *beasted* and ended up 'getting wet in the ogin'. (*Beasting* is UK military slang used by soldiers when one is physically punished for doing something unacceptable, usually involving a series of physical training exercises.) Getting wet in the ogin (a large body of water including the sea or ocean) meant we were to fully submerge into a water tank with kit on including your weapon.

This kind of treatment went on repeatedly to the point of mental and physical exhaustion. Getting beasted and wet only meant one thing: you spent more time cleaning your rifle when you could have been resting. No one wanted to be that guy who puts others in such a painful position. As a body of men, we were attuned to working together and mindful of what we were being taught.

By and large, no matter how fierce, storms don't last forever,. Winds might blow hard, and life can get tough, but sooner or later it subsides. Even though the commando training was physically and mentally challenging, it left one feeling proud and confident upon finishing. We should realise that life can be ruthless and often bewildering, causing even the most balanced, focused, and well-intended person to stray from his or her chosen way. At one point you might have lived with passion and excitement, clearly recognising all your unique strengths and focussed beliefs—only to have your experiences blur your dreams. What you should know is that life is not fair, so do not be surprised when it treats you unfairly.

To a higher degree, the fear of failing has caused people to stop trying. It is by the same token that many have failed to tap into the unlimited potential that is within them until the day they breathe their last. Bruce Lee once said, "Like everyone else, you want to learn the way to win, but never to accept the way to lose". Even though no one plans to fail, you have to be prepared to experience failure one way or another.

If success is what we need and aspire to, we should not be afraid to fail. Instead, we should be afraid to *not* try. American journalist Norman Cousins said, "The tragedy of life is not death, but what we let die inside of us while we live".[63] Do not be a dead person walking.

FACING YOUR INNER DEMONS

When it comes to confronting inner demons, many hardly do. Dealing with our inner demons is a reality, and how we choose to undertake them is determined when they

---

[63] https://www.dailypioneer.com/2015/columnists/meaning-of-a-full-life.html#:~:text=This%20is%20what%20Norman%20Cousins,importantly%20the%20way%20they%20die.

transpire. In this chapter, inner demons are referred to as fears, which we harbour within ourselves. Fear can be natural and work towards the advantage of those who accept and administer it properly.

Adversity introduces us to our true selves. At some point, we will all encounter conditions that go beyond our physical and mental prowess. Like most of us, I grew up embracing my own fears, one of which is swimming. Water scared me to death, and learning how to swim while well advanced in age was not a simple undertaking. It was almost impossible to pass the Royal Marines battle swimming test (RMBST).

The fear of jumping into the deep end of the pool nearly cost my friend Marvin Opoku and me our chance of joining the Royal Marines commandos. This swim test was a pass-or-fail moment we had to undergo in order to make it on to the course. The test involved jumping from a 3-metre diving board into a 3.5-metre swimming pool while wearing a full kit carrying webbing weighing twelve pounds, and a rifle of nine pounds, a total of twenty-one pounds.

Upon resurfacing, we had to swim thirty metres to the edge of the pool and then hand over our kit whilst treading water, without touching the sides. After handing over the kit unaided, we were meant to continue treading water for two minutes. The whole process lasted five minutes, the worst five minutes I've ever experienced as a non-swimmer.

Being the only two people of our kind and coming from a non-swimming background joining the elite forces was unimaginable at this stage for my friend and me, but we strongly believed and reminded ourselves to never lose heart or to fall into despair. Unequivocally, as believers, we knew and told ourselves we were going to triumph.

I have learnt that if you want anything badly enough, you will always get it. This is to say, whatever you set your mind to conceive, you will surely achieve it, mostly if you want it on another level. We really wanted to pass the swimming test so badly in order to pass the commando course, even badly enough that we had to face our fear in the pool every day during swimming lessons.

It took us a couple of months of sweating in the pool and consuming litres of chlorine water before we all finally passed the Royal Marines Battle Swimming Test. It was from the countless hours of determination and resilience we invested in the pool that what we thought impossible then became possible. Truly, no matter the struggles we face, or the problems that lie across our path, we shall always find ways to reach our biggest dreams if only we remain persistent towards those goals.

Zig Ziglar said, "F-E-A-R: has two meanings: Forget Everything and Run or Face Everything and Rise. The choice is yours".[64] Unfortunately, while to a large degree this is true, the concept of facing demons will vary. While what works well for one might be disastrous for another, the key to unlocking the door to our inner fears cannot be opened by any other key than the inner self alone. There is no master key; in other words, how one approaches one's inner dialogue differs from another. No one size fits all.

OVERCOMING YOUR FEARS

When dealing with our inner fears, we must have a *never say die* attitude. We must not stop at anything; our fears should no longer be in control of us. In Chinese, this philosophy is called Mo Chih Chu, a samurai term that means 'moving straight ahead without hesitation'.

There is a Zen poem attributed to famous Japanese swordsman Miyamoto Musashi,[65] which says,

> Under the sword lifted high
> There is hell making you tremble.
> But go ahead,
> And you have the land of bliss.

People have been incarcerated in their own mental prisons through self-doubts and regrets, blinded by the notion that nothing is wrong inside them. Most of our fears stem from our *what ifs*.

We tend to worry about the repercussions of what might happen tomorrow, instead of focusing on what should be done today. The what if mentality has killed many people's dreams more than failure itself has. If you can get rid of the what if mentality, you will be able to overcome your inner fears.

The moment you begin to face your fears, you will start to realise they are not as big as you had thought they were. It is when you don't turn around to face them head-on that you see them loom as big and scary. Most of the time, the longer you avoid your fears, the bigger and stronger they grow and take root in your mind.

---

[64] https://medium.com/@kristarausin/f-e-a-r-has-two-meanings-forget-everything-and-run-or-face-everything-and-rise-bb5c8dd676fc#:~:text=Save-,%E2%80%9CF%2DE%2DA%2DR%3A%20has%20two%20meanings%3A%20Forget%20Everything%20And%20Run%20or,is%20yours.%E2%80%9D%20%E2%80%94%20Zig%20Ziglar.

[65] https://www.goodreads.com/quotes/48712-under-the-sword-lifted-high-there-is-hell-making-you

Growing up in an impoverished environment, I discovered that it is not only the lack of opportunities that cause failure amongst many people. Fear paralysis is a major factor contributing to failure. We become paralysed with our own fears and for the fear of what we think the outcome might be. We side track ourselves, neglecting our dreams because we are afraid.

Learning from her background and writing career, British author JK Rowling said in her Harvard commencement address, "Some failure is inevitable. It is impossible to live without failing at something unless you live so cautiously that you might as well not have lived at all".[66]

It is OK to feel afraid and fail at some point; keep in mind that failure is part of the process of success. When you fail, do not let failure paralyse you from trying again. Life has many options. *You* need to forge ahead.

There's an old story told about a man so afraid of the sight of his shadow and the sound of his footsteps that he ran away from them. But the more he ran, the faster the footsteps sounded and the more swiftly his shadow followed. Falling into panic, he ran faster and faster until he died of exhaustion.

He didn't realise that if he'd only stopped running, what he feared would stop chasing him. Resting in the shade by a tree would make the shadow disappear and the footsteps cease.

The moral behind this story is that, like many, we run from ourselves; if only we stop running from our inner fears, they too will cease to torment us. Resting in greater understanding and knowing of the self, we will no longer be frightened by our fears. We will embrace and overcome them. Learn to acknowledge your fear. And under no circumstances should you sweep and hide it under a rug. Face it instead.

THE NEED FOR COURAGE

Courage is an element that, if properly understood, can lead to success; it is the quality everyone should cultivate in order to get huge dividends over the long run. But if not taken seriously, a lack of courage can make people give up on their dreams. The first Israeli prime minister, David Ben-Gurion, stated, "Courage is a special kind of knowledge: the knowledge of how to fear what ought to be feared and how not to fear what ought not to be feared".[67]

---

[66] https://www.jkrowling.com/harvard-commencement-address/.
[67] https://www.brainyquote.com/quotes/david_bengurion_121138.

Courage is not the absence of fear but rather the triumph over it. Hence, the brave person is not the one who does not feel afraid but the one who conquers fear. The anatomy of fear is that, like any other creation, it is your own creation.

Our beliefs alone without courage will not bring any effect; but if coupled with courage, our beliefs will stimulate the body's action into acquiring our aspirations. The degree of our courage if on par with our beliefs will ultimately determine the amount of achievement we get out of life.

If fully tapped into, courage can help one persist where others have failed. A person of courage is never afraid. Whatever goals and dreams you have, do not be scared to pursue them, but be determined and have the courage to push forward.

As it is one of the core values practiced in the military, courage is seen to have massively assisted people to accomplish goals and overcome difficulties. Timidity, on the other hand, can crush our dreams and expectations.

Courage can be expressed in different ways, such as starting a business or asking for a loved one's hand in marriage. Often, we see that just like life itself, every minute of our existence requires our ability to employ courage. It is the same reason much is not achieved by many people: their lack of courage.

This also applies to soldiers who not only need courage to fight on the battlefield but to excel in other aspects of life. Similarly, other than fighting in battle, involving ourselves in activities like physical training every day will test and enhance levels of courage. Moreover, excessive physical training will sharpen internal and external spheres, which eventually build an overall strong fighting spirit. Such being the case, it is obligatory that soldiers must indulge in physical training to cultivate robust mental and physical stamina. Gradually, through hard work and persistence, we begin to attain levels of fitness we never thought we could. And by overcoming physical pain and suffering, we develop minds and bodies that are well trained and indestructible.

I recall one morning in Lympstone, during a hard physical training session, feeling like my heart was going to be ripped out of my chest. I was at the brink of collapse from exhaustion when a colleague suddenly rushed towards me. After seeing me staggering for balance, he held me by the shoulders and slowly walked me out of the training grounds.

By then, little twinkling stars had already filled my eyes and blurred my vision. I sat down for a couple of minutes and drank some water as I recovered. Upon regaining a clear head, the session had already finished. I stood up silently and dragged myself back to the dormitory with the rest of the troop. Franklin Roosevelt said, "A smooth sea never made a skilled sailor".[68] The commando course was as tough as steel nails yet at the same time enjoyable. And due to its distinct and formidable type of physical training, the course demanded courage and determination to a really high degree.

As a result of being thoroughly subjected to relentless pressure and scrutiny, we took the bull by the horns. The mindset to maintain our core purpose and determination in the face of dramatically changed circumstances allowed us to not only overcome setbacks but to press forward.

The mentality of pushing through pain and suffering was one of the prominent lessons cultivated in the early physical training days in Lympstone. This mindset was only achieved by constantly toiling above and beyond one's limits and breaking points. Often, the instructors tailored the sessions in such a way that they tested our spirits and made our stay there a living hell.

As slow as a tortoise, a day passed like a week, a week like a month. And the only hope to survive was hard work. But guess what? When frequently wet and tired, your mind loses focus; fear and doubt start to creep in, which is when a true fighter or commando is born, strong, and emerging out of adversity with a smile.

It was in these painful and difficult moments that I started employing the SLAPP (stop, locate clue, activate imagery, park, perform) method. It has always worked for me beyond a reasonable doubt.

STOP

Sometimes on our way, things go haywire. But what do you do to get past that? When things get rough, stop whatever you're doing and take a deep breath while sorting yourself out. For example, you might be on a run or any physical training session that turns out to be challenging and makes you feel like you want to quit. For a few seconds, stop and calm yourself down. Control your breathing and slow down if you must, but make sure you do not quit.

You do not need to be the strongest or the fastest to always win over life's changes. Remember, winning isn't always about finishing first. Sometimes, winning is just a matter of finishing.

---

[68] https://www.quotespedia.org/authors/f/franklin-d-roosevelt/a-smooth-sea-never-made-a-skilled-sailor-franklin-d-roosevelt/.

You might be struggling with something, but as long as you do not stop trying, you will be way ahead and better than the person who quits every time shit hits the fan.

Similarly, in today's busy world, we must learn to slow down, to stop and adjust our lives accordingly towards our goals and dreams. Do you know why it is vital to know where you are going in life? If you do, are you then walking in the correct direction of your dreams? Think of it this way: when you know where you are going, you will prepare in advance for any detours and unexpected distractions.

In this case, stopping does not necessarily mean ceasing all action or sabotaging progress. This means stepping back to evaluate the situation from a different perspective. In military terms, this process is called *regrouping*, also known as *reorganising*. The fact is when you hit a wall and feel like giving up, remember to regroup. This could mean having a word with yourself—that is, asking yourself what you did right and what you did wrong—to simply strategise your goals. You could as well seek help from others.

On your journey towards the attainment of success, life presents itself with twists and turns. It is your responsibility to choose how to respond to such turns. Remember, when you stop does not mean you have come to an end of everything. *End* is not that you have come to the end of your dreams or career. Rather, *end* means you have comprehended that your "effort never dies". Your efforts properly aligned with your beliefs will never go to waste.

LOCATE CLUE

While it may occur as a revelation to those of us who are facing struggles, the answer to virtually all our problems resides within us. This second stage allows you to understand your behaviours (strengths and weaknesses). Often, you need to go within yourself to see what you are made of.

American Navy SEAL David Goggins, retired, said, "Everybody comes to a point in their life when they want to quit. But it's what you do at that moment that determines who you are".[69]

You must ask yourself if you are the person who always quits when things get tough or if you are that person who always pushes forward regardless of how dark and painful it gets. If you fail, which you will occasionally do, you must never quit, because to FAIL only means one thing: *first attempt in learning*. You might have failed your first time, the second time,

---

[69]   https://www.azquotes.com/quote/823377#:~:text=point%20in...-,Everybody%20comes%20to%20a%20point%20in%20their%20life%20when%20they,that%20determines%20who%20you%20are.

and even the third, but no matter how many times you fail. you must remain focused and persistent and keep trying until what you seek is within your reach. Use failure to learn what works and what doesn't. Just don't quit.

ACTIVATE IMAGERY

Do you sometimes wonder why you do certain things? When you ask yourself this question, your mind instantly launches its indestructible weapons and goes to war for you. It begins with creating images and possibilities that will help you achieve particular things. This also applies to your goals and dreams, which you must routinely (daily) visualise in order for them to be manifested into their physical form.

You must visualise the kind of world you want to live in by dreaming about the life you want to accomplish. Dream about the kind of person you want to become after achieving success, according to your own definition of success. They say the world is your oyster; why not make the most of it?

The power of visualisation allows us to act as if we have already achieved what we set out to accomplish. We need to endlessly rehearse success in our minds. We should imagine exactly how we will be after we accomplish our dreams. This is how, by constantly thinking about how we want to be, we ultimately program our minds to make us what we want.

Visualisation is daydreaming with an authentic purpose, and in this case, our purpose is making sure we attain our accomplishments. Be advised that just because it appears impossible does not mean it can never be achieved.

What images are you activating in your mind today? What is it that you can see in your mind's eye?

What you must know is

Decisions

Your decisions,
Not conditions,
Determine your manifestations.

Your perception,
As well as expectation,
Bring about transformation.

Decide now what you want tomorrow,
And everything else will follow.

PARK

Have you ever been under pressure to the extent that your brain runs like wildfire? Many of us have. When you are under pressure and feel like you are going to die, your mind starts to play tricks on you, sometimes to the point of completely shutting you down. It is during these distressing moments where you need to have conversations with your inner self in order to remain persistent. In the process of doing that, learn to clear the negativity that your mind harbours.

When it comes to the value of persistence, one of my favourite power thoughts comes from former US president Calvin Coolidge, who asserted:

> Nothing in the world can take the place of persistence. Talent will not; nothing is more common than unsuccessful men with talent. Genius will not; unrewarded genius is almost a proverb. Education will not; the world is full of educated derelicts. Persistence and determination alone are omnipotent. The slogan Press On! has solved and always will solve the problems of the human race.[70]

Time and again, we are going to find ourselves in situations over our heads, sometimes making it difficult or impossible for us. But what you should know is that no matter what, no matter how, you must press on! Everything we are capable or incapable of achieving flows from what we have decided within that sphere called the mind. The only place all our dreams and aspirations become possible or impossible is in our own thinking. All we want is within the proximity of our minds.

So why do many fail to utilise this opportunity of turning their impossibilities into possibilities? Surely this all comes down to how they have programmed their minds and belief systems.

PERFORM

This stage of SLAPP will catapult you to the tip of your performance. The process helps you do whatever you set yourself to do in the correct order and with professionalism. How

---

[70]   https://www.washburn.edu/student-life/recreation-wellness/employee-wellness/documents/EW-OC-Persistence.pdf.

do you improve on your weaknesses? Do you lie down and talk your way out? Or do you go out and do what needs to be done? There is no substitute for hard work.

All that you can achieve and fail to achieve is a direct result of your own efforts. To that end, you won't win or achieve success through a back door or without effort. The secret to becoming a first-class performer resides in ultimate practice, so put in the work! Nevertheless, no matter how tough or impossible a task might appear to be, remember to always aim to go past your expected capabilities. Keep working hard and test your limits, and even when you accomplish what you wanted, push even further and harder than before.

Carefully meditate on these words: when you think you've given all you can give, strive to give just a little bit more. Often, the very last key that hangs on a ring is the one that will open the door.

The point to grasp and absorb is that anything worth achieving is worth striving for. Achieving greatness is not an easy task. It requires hard work, strenuous effort, focus, and persistence. However, the extra effort that you can employ when faced with adversity, or when you're at the very tip where you feel like giving up, is the very effort that will change the story of your life.

The only way to get to the next level is by striving to do more than what you've always done. This attitude will not only stretch you out of your comfort zone but also mean all the difference in the world.

Making it to the commando phase was a huge success. It not only reshaped and strengthened my mindset, it broadened my physical fitness horizons such that whatever I set my mind to do, I pursue it with a positive attitude. I do not limit myself to impossibilities nor easily give in to defeat when faced with adversity. I always fight and never call quits.

Adapt the SLAPP method and constantly use it. However, do not only apply it in your physical training sessions but in all aspects of your life. Circumstances, as they say, do not make a person, they only reveal his or her character. So when things get rough, as they always do, remember to SLAPP your challenges.

IN PURSUIT OF A BETTER LIFE

To aim at the medium, emulate the highest, thus even if one is willing to be but a superior man, he should attempt to become a sage. The level of personality and character one can attain depends upon the effort one makes.
—Confucius

My days in Malawi were warm and beautiful. However, on 22 October it was time to answer destiny's call and take a leap of faith. This was the day I had to leave for the United Kingdom; a lot of emotions flooded the atmosphere, albeit it was a thrilling, blissful, and memorable day.

Family members and friends accompanied me to the airport where I was to board a plane to a foreign land. Truth be told, it was a tough moment for me to accept that I was going away. I would miss family and friends. On my departure, I exchanged hugs and kisses with relatives in sorrow. Being the head of my family and its breadwinner, I noticed that most of my family members were concerned about my departure. As we bid farewell and parted ways, I noticed my parents' looks, thinking I was going into exile. But I perceived my trip to the United Kingdom as a step toward success.

As a man, I pretended not to have noticed their concerns as I gathered false courage within myself and remained unfazed. Yet deep down in my heart, I shed tears uncontrollably. I organised myself and then remained calm and strong. When it was time for take-off, the emotion changed, and I was beaming with more confidence than any time before.

My trip to the United Kingdom was a vivid breakthrough I had anticipated for many years, which I had to pursue. My emotions drew me closer to the dream I had been harbouring. In my mind I saw an ecstatic moment filled with euphoria.

Then I realised I was not just boarding an airplane to a foreign land but to another height that would promote my life. The more I ascended the aircraft's stairs, the more I knew my life was drifting towards meaningful change. The trip provided me with time to visualise my new future and meditate on possible challenges. I was not merely getting on board but was provided with a special moment of visualising and meditating.

Surprisingly, the inexplicable excitement that conquered my ego made it difficult for me to notice minor details of events happening around me. As I entered the cabin, I heard a charming voice. I noticed a female, dark-skinned flight attendant, a young Ethiopian lady in her late twenties. She welcomed me aboard. I sank into my comfortable seat and tried to organise myself. All that happened looked like a dream. I couldn't wait to be in London to start living up to my expectations. That's when I knew my abstract power of belief was now at its milking stage and being manifested and acted upon. Though I was not yet in London, the fact that I was on the plane that was taking me to my dream land made me see my life changing for the better. My mind was already in the United Kingdom, pursuing my life-long goals. It was a blissful moment, filled with heart-warming voices and melodies. I prayed earnestly when the plane took off, leaving Kamuzu International Airport and heading towards my final destination. I asked God in my prayer to grant me intelligence that suffuses life. I reminded the Creator about the beautiful and ugly days of my life in Africa. I also asked him to give me better ways of becoming great while in the foreign land. I felt so glad about the conversation I had with God that on several occasions I reminded myself that I was in a plane flying away from poverty. It is fair to say I was walking on air at that moment.

Then I remembered Albert Einstein's words: "Imagination is everything. It is the preview of life's coming attractions".[71] I allowed my imagination to roam freely. (Lack of imagination is one thing that prevents many people from realising their potential.). Our opportunities are essentially limited by our own imaginations. If we want to become great in life, we must utilise our imagination to the fullest. One of the core beliefs I have embraced and adapted over the years is setting up goals and then believing I would certainly find a way of giving life to them.

The best example of activities I personally acted upon with belief was the day I applied to the British army. The decision was founded on determination. I had to go through several ups and downs to achieve my desires. It was possible for me to give up my efforts of becoming a British soldier upon realising there were many people I knew who tried but never succeeded. However, I still knew from the bottom of my heart that my application to the British armed forces would pass. I am happy most things are possible with me just because I believe in what I do.

This does not essentially come from my wishful thinking but through training my perception of things and actions. I have always told myself that I can bring to life things I think about and that it doesn't matter where one comes from, their race or their background, if one wishes to accomplish one's desires. The only things that matter are you and what you believe in. If you believe in limitations to what you can achieve, then that will become your reality. All the people who believe in themselves should be ready to take risks. Many have risen from nonentities to big shots in societies and from hopelessness to success because they believed.

Rise and Shine

I shall rise and shine
Towards the dark blue skies and not whine.
Believe me, when I cross that frontier line
Your love shall ride into mine.
Indeed, and in need, this will be our time.

---

[71] https://www.brainyquote.com/quotes/albert_einstein_384440.

I shall rise beyond the blue skies,
Treading orbits where dead men tell no lies.
Fathomless meditating with my broken,
Whacked will be my limits being broken,
For before him I shall bow down to hearken.

I shall at all costs never cease to shine,
Even with the slightest taste of wine.
If life's turmoil or vicissitudes take over,
God's grace shall be upon me to cover.

I shall believe and perceive,
For a moment where I shall receive
Where not only gaining big muscles
Will help winning big tussles,
But also where good brains
Will produce good grains.

I shall rise and dine
With the wise and fine.
Above all calamities,
Will make use of all opportunities.

I shall rise and fight
Neither with a weapon or flight
But ultimately with my own verity
And completely with nobody's authority.

LIFE IN SERVICE

In pursuit of one's vision, focus and determination are of paramount importance. The first step towards fulfilling one's purpose is being strong-minded. Determination to create the world one wants is essential in achieving success. While trying to create one's own planet, one should neglect other people's perceptions of life. Every person was created to achieve distinct purposes, even if we sometimes imitate other people. This might be the reason why I joined the British armed forces while it was impossible for others. Unlike many who joined the British army for personal financial freedom, I joined for other reasons, such as growing in my career and to evolve into a limitless being. It is important to realise that sometimes we are limited by our environment. However, contrary to common perceptions, one does not need to be at the right place at the right time to become successful, since progress might sometimes come if one does the right thing with the right frame of mind.

It was a difficult decision to abandon all I had accomplished in Malawi, but I believed in the skill I possessed. And the more I expected to grow, I accepted I had to leave everything. I perceived myself as a big fish in a small pond, and change at this stage was inevitable, so I had to try a new environment. Associate professor of ethics and philosophy and author Ronald Osborn wrote, "Undertake something that is difficult; it will do you good. Unless you try to do something beyond what you have already mastered, you will never grow"[72]. The British army became the shark I wanted to swim with and the ocean I wanted to grow in. However, it is one thing to have potential and another to realise it. The army has elevated my life to the level where I can fulfil most of my desires. Life in the army is tough and challenging.

It is a test for both the mind and the body, yet the benefits that have transpired to my mental, physical, and financial portfolios are unthinkable.

Like most soldiers who fight against injustice as well as for their countries, we fight our own individual internal battles. Overcoming these battles becomes a stepping stone towards achieving greatness. Ralph Waldo Emerson says, "What lies before us and what lies behind us are tiny matters if compared to what lies within us"[73]. As human beings, we need to understand that there is no barrier, before or behind us. We are empowered to become whatever we believe in, but only if we believe. Generally, those who don't achieve their life desires are those who don't believe. One needs to believe to achieve great things. A man without belief is like a painkiller without relief.

People from different nations and ethnic backgrounds ought to be treated equally. Life in the army is really amazing. Making friends for life is an extreme resource inasmuch as greatness is concerned. Through the military I discovered that association with people who have the right impact and influence helps one climb the ladder of success. Like in the army, success is not just a dream come true but a dream made true. We are made to be what we are. In order to be successful, never wait for the moment when your dreams shall come true; get out there, take some calculated risks, and make your dreams a reality.

No one but yourself will make dreams come true. The saying that greatness is not just a heritage, it is an attainment is true. I have acquired much during my military service,

---

72   https://www.googlereads.com/quotes/1347729-undertake-something-that-is-difficult-it-will-do-you-good
73   https://srtklaw.com/thought/what-lies-behind-us-and-what-lies-before-us-are-tiny-matters-compared-to-what-lies-within-us-ralph-waldo-emerson/

which has contributed enormously to my success. One important thing I always loved is boot cleaning. I usually do this in the evening.

Unlike some who might look at boot cleaning as a simple activity, I see the same as a meaningful and educative art. Every time I carry my boots and polish them with a brush, I feel like renewing my heart and preparing it for new tasks.

In a true soldier's spirit or wisdom, one needs to have a pure and clean soul to be effective. Cleaning my boots became a sure way of cleansing doubts and fears. Like the soul and the body that can't work in isolation, my boots are part of my life and I'm equally part of them. Boot polishing has allowed me to go into a state of open-mindedness, and such moments have enabled me to go into some formless and dimensionless spheres. However, it is also in such spheres that my patience has been fully ignited.

How one thinks determines how one lives. And one's perception determines the manifestation of one's destiny. Apart from being every soldier's perception to become the best, the British army has really prepared me for higher expectations. During basic training, one thing that remained clear to me was that not all fights fought on the battlefield come without their own challenges, but it is up to the individuals to decide where to take life's blows to. Generally, military training was tough and yet a celebrated tussle for me.

Serving in one of the best armies in the world has taught me several valuable lessons, including learning to utilise inert abilities and resources at one's disposal. I believe in turning big dreams into reality. We can never achieve greatness if we don't perceive it inside ourselves. All the training I have acquired has not only shaped my physical being but enhanced my inner perception. Furthermore, I love the fact that the British army provides big opportunities for everyone to showcase their talents and become what they want to be.

We Were Soldiers

Highly anticipated and divine was the moment
Family and friends celebrated.
Reminisced are the days of hard, sweet pain,
When thoughts fast accelerated like a train.

Those long and beautiful days came with the cold,
But we marched blissfully and boldly.
Daytimes we toiled throughout,
and nights came, with all of us in bed tired.

As advocates we had to go to the extreme,
So we pushed firmly beyond proximity.

Talents and skills were ultimately identified,
For highly appreciated they were quantified.
Our lives as new lads were full of scarcity.
Robust, we now merrily serve with prosperity.

Discrete and remarkable,
We were respected,
Yet the best was significantly expected.
Surely those early morning discoveries
Have paved the way for our great recoveries.
It was a profound and gruelling transition.
But at least everyone has found a position.

Perfectly conducted was our true integrity.
Worthwhile earned at last is our true dignity.
For all the runs we had in a mile
Have today proven to be worthwhile.
Such exclusive ecstasy herein we now find.
All we needed to do was endure in the mind.

9

THE PURPOSE
OF LIFE

The purpose of life is to live a life of purpose.
—Isaac Bashevis Singer

Oftentimes we ask ourselves what the purpose of life is, yet only a few are able to grasp and understand its authentic meaning. What use is life without purpose?

Finding the purpose or meaning of one's life comes from within; it is a process that comes from a substantial introspection and vivid understanding of oneself. You will never find the purpose of your life by becoming an imposter of someone's purpose, you must be you in order to find yourself and your own purpose.

Surely, our lives and the world we live in are only temporary and in a state of change; one must become one with the self, leading oneself to a realisation of truth and purpose. For only through themselves will people be able to discover their purpose. It is important to know that finding the purpose of your life is in line with your goals, personality, and passion.

To have no purpose is to live a non-purposeful life. The true purpose of life can be greatly understood by ultimately meditating on the words of Paramahansa Yogananda, an Indian Hindu monk who said, "When we are born we are crying whilst the world rejoices; we must live our lives in such a way that when we die the world cries whilst we are rejoicing"[74].

What these worlds are trying to teach us is that we should live a life of purpose, a life that not only benefits us but considers others as well.

The main purpose of life is to serve humanity, and to leave this world a little better than you found it, according to Sir Robert Baden-Powell, the founder of the Boy Scouts.[75]

It is one thing to have a purpose yet another to fulfil it, but either way, in order to fulfil your purpose, you have to take aim. In verse 7 of the *Tao Te Ching*, Laozi said, "Serve the needs of others and all your own needs will be fulfilled. Through selfless action, fulfilment is attained".[76]

LIVING A DASH-ORIENTED LIFE

When it comes to living a meaningful life—thus, analysing the core purpose of our existence—we should all learn these pronounced and enlightening words by American poet Kevin Welch: "There will be two dates on your tombstone and all your friends will read 'em but all that's going to matter is that little dash between 'em"[77].

---

[74]   https://www.googlereads.com/author/quotes/14650.parahansa_yogananda

[75]   https://www.azquotes.com/author/759-Robert_Baden_Powell.

[76]   https://renewyourmind.co.za/service-step-12-serve-the-needs-of-others-and-all-your-own-needs-will-be-fulfilled/.

[77]   https://quotefancy.com/quote/1608950/Kevin-Welch-There-ll-be-two-dates-on-your-tombstone-and-all-your-friends-will-read-em-but

Hits the nail on the head, right? Whatever path you've chosen has considerable meaning to you and should be memorialised in such a way that others will forever remember you for it.

As far as serving your life with purpose is concerned, this is really of vital importance. That little dash, the small horizontal line crossing between the date you were born and the date you died, symbolises your whole life. Some of you are sceptical and probably thinking, *My whole life in a dash?*

Time and again we should ask ourselves how we wish to be remembered, decades after we are long gone. Such introspective dialogues should include the kind of legacy we are going to leave behind and how we want our names to be remembered.

On one remarkable early morning, sitting quietly in my study and perusing through the pages of *Live Your Dash* by Linda Ellis, I came across her inspiring poem, "The Dash".[78] Here's a small piece of it:

> I read of a man who stood to speak
> At the funeral of a friend.
> He referred to the dates on the tombstone
> From the beginning … to the end.
>
> He noted that first came the date of birth
> And spoke the following date with tears,
> But he said what mattered most of all
> Was the dash between those years.

Apart from being a world-famous poem, I find it to be one of the greatest. Vast and unparalleled with its meticulous meaning, the poem prolifically changed my perception of living life as well as cherishing every moment. Above all, it taught me lessons on how to live a dash-oriented life.

As an individual, how are you living your dash? If you might happen to die today, right now, what influence will your dash bring to mankind? What impact will it create? What would the world and its future generations remember you for? Would you die knowing you've lived a great and fulfilling life, or you would die with remorse and shame? By honestly answering these questions, you will begin to discover the true meaning of life and utterly accomplish its purpose, therefore maximising your dash. Without a doubt,

---

[78] https://lifeism.co/the-dash-poem-by-linda-ellis#the-dash-poem-by-linda-ellis.

how you choose to live your dash is ultimately your own choice. However, it is imperative to live your dash (life) in such a way that it is worth remembering.

You are the creator of your own story. You're in control of its narrative and how you want others to remember the life you lived. One thing to always remember is that years after you are gone, people should read about you. A carefully curated lifetime of memories should be accumulated for others to cherish later, when you are dead and gone. This can be anything left behind that tells the world a complete story of your life, goals, dreams, failures, and accomplishments.

For a moment, sit somewhere quiet and relax, close your eyes, and ask yourself how you wish to be remembered as a parent. As a brother or sister. As a friend. As a manager or leader? In general terms, how do you want to be remembered as a human being?

Well, in any case, you are not supposed to live and die without anyone knowing that you ever existed. Even the scripture pinpoints that, "A good name is more desirable than riches, and loving favour than silver and gold"[79]. This is to say you will be remembered not by the amount of worth you accumulate or the riches in your possession but by what you leave behind in the hearts and minds of others. Now, ask yourself, what can you leave in the minds and hearts of others that will always be remembered?

Your name, together with your beliefs, courage, victory, and how you lived should be the fuel that ignites the burning desire in others to believe in the fullness of their destiny. As Abraham Lincoln said, "In the end, it's not the years in your life that counts. It's the life in your years".[80] Are you giving life to your years?

THE POINT OF AIM (POA)

Like in the armed forces, when we were taught to shoot, you need to have a point of aim (POA). This is a point you aim at when you are shooting at targets. The point of aim (POA) remains with you throughout but only changes when there is a change in range, such as if you are shooting long or short ranges.

In comparison to life, we all have goals and targets that we aim at, be it in academics or sports, relationships, and even accumulating riches. But bear in mind, to achieve these goals one has got to stay committed and focused, ensuring that this point always remains the same or adjusted according to its concurrent conditions.

---

[79]   https://www.geneva.edu/blog/biblical-wisdom/proverbs-22-1
[80]   https://www.quotespedia.org/authors/a/abraham-lincoln/in-the-end-its-not-the-years-in-your-life-that-counts-its-the-life-in-your-years-abraham-lincoln/.

MAINTAINING YOUR POINT OF AIM

One thing I have come to terms with is that few things are achieved by most people because many live a life defined by imaginary limits. Nowadays, people think once they have reached a certain level of respect, status, influence, or success that they have finally made it or reached the purpose of life. Truth be told, life is like an imaginary long game played without a referee or scoreboard, and it does not end until your death.

To keep scoring on life's scoreboard, there is a need to maintain your point of aim (POA). The moment you change your aim is the moment you start missing your targets and hitting where not necessary.

Success, on the other hand, does not mean you will always attain your goals, but if you remain disciplined and persevere towards achieving those goals, sooner or later you will find yourself on the right path leading to success. "Our plans miscarry because they have no aim. When a man does not know what harbour he is making for, no wind is the right wind".—Seneca[81]

---

[81] https://www.brainyquote.com/quotes/lucius_annaeus_seneca_155011.

10

AS YOU THINK,
SO SHALL YOU BE

As a man thinketh in his heart so is he.
Psalm 23:7

WHO ARE YOU?

Have you asked yourself this question? Often, people get really confused about who they really are authentically to what they are fashionably. This is a question of nothingness versus something, unimaginable contrast between proportionate levels of spirituality and physicality.

When introducing ourselves, we usually define who we are as what we do: "My name is John. I'm a doctor". It is not what we look like (appearance), or what we do (occupation) that brings a bona fide meaning and purpose to life but rather who we really are. *The Power of Belief* teaches us to see beyond categories. To a greater extent, who we are is more than what we do.

According to human nature, who we are is not expounded by what society has typified and bounded us with. Who we are is a manifestation of an invisible and infinite self that is within our body, call it emptiness or nothingness. This emptiness or nothingness that occupies our physical form is beyond measure and cannot be characterised by words or illustrated with symbols. Confined to a body of flesh, blood, and bones, the emptiness is best understood upon realising that as spiritual beings we are a soul with a body, not a body with a soul.

Though its nature and existence are beyond illustrations, description, and language, we have resolved to define who we truly are by identifications and vocations, yet we are more than these titles. Who we truly are is somehow like water: nameless, shapeless, and formless.

In the same way that the components of a tree (roots, leaves, bark, and branches) do not constitute a tree, man is not the exterior mechanism of his bodily parts (blood, bones, and flesh). According to Lao Tzu, what really makes a man be a man and a tree to be a tree is a limitless life force imperceptible and invisibly within, eluding all the five senses[82].

As a distinct portion of success, knowing who we are is of great significance. Often, what we see when we look in the mirror is not actually who we really are. Instead, who we are is the nothingness that lies under our human figure. The reflection replicates the person perceived but does not define the nature of that person and who he or she really is. Our perceptions determine our manifestations but not our real selves.

---

[82]   https://shadowhabitat.org/a-parable-for-wetlands/

STOP STOPPING YOURSELF

Throughout my life and military career, I've always reminded myself and others not to stop at anything, no matter how hard or impossible a situation may seem. This attitude of not settling has seen me through hard times and helped me accelerate to the top of the ladder. Where there's a will, as I've learnt, there is always a way. Do not allow your doubts and fears to stop you from becoming the person you are meant to be. You are unstoppable, so stop stopping yourself. Believe it and you're almost there. You are your own biggest obstacle, so step aside and do not stand in your own way. Walking through the corridors of one of the offices of the Royal Marines commando, I came across a poem by Walter D Wintle.[83]

The words inspired me and profoundly uplifted my morale in such a manner that augmented a positive attitude towards all my days there.

"The Man Who Thinks He Can"

If you think you are beaten, you are.
If you think you dare not, you don't.
If you'd like to win, but think you can't,
It's almost certain you won't.

[...]

Life's battles don't always go
To the faster or stronger man;
But soon or later, the man who wins
Is the man who thinks he can.

I wrote the poem on a piece of paper, which I later put on my locker in front of my bed. Each time I woke in the morning I spent at least a couple of minutes going through the lines. It then became my daily routine to read it each time we went through our day-to-day endeavours, mostly during the arduous physical training we received from our physical training instructors.

All things considered, by pushing on through pain and suffering, I was well informed. It is through these lessons that I've managed to learn more about myself. In moments of adversity, it's always worth testing our breaking points, for only then will we be introduced to our true selves. Sometimes, all the doubts, fears, and biases you have are just you against

---

[83] https://rainydaypoems.com/poems-for-kids/inspirational-poems/the-man-who-thinks-he-can-walter-d-wintle/ .

yourself. The only way to get rid of them is to conquer yourself. Once you learn to conquer yourself, there is nothing that can stop you. Confucius said, "He who conquers himself is the mightiest warrior".

Challenges will always be in our lives but always remember the words of Napoleon Hill: "You can be anything you want to be, if only you can believe with sufficient conviction and act in accordance with your faith; for whatever the mind can conceive and believe, it can achieve".[84]Never allow your challenges to become barriers to your dreams. Above all, "Do not limit your challenges; challenge your limits". —Jerry Dunn.[85]

From time to time life will push us into a corner of pain, squeezing us so harshly out of our comfort zones, stretching us to unthinkable levels, and even forcing us to accept defeat. Robert Schuller said, "Tough times never last but tough people do"[86]. You will never know how strong you are until being strong is the only option, so don't throw in the towel before the fight.

Inasmuch as we all possibly know, there is an epic dream within us waiting to be birthed, but this only becomes attainable if we unveil the mask of counterfeit. Virtually, there is no limit as to how far we can go or any mountain too big to climb if we don't stand in the way of our dreams. Perhaps the only thing that will stop us from becoming the best there could ever be is ourselves. Stop stopping yourself and become the person you were created to be.

Our lives are like an open book with a story revealing to the world its author. Being the author of our own stories, we should ask ourselves how we can inspire the world. What kind of world would this be if all people were the same? No one will be interested to hear stories about people who gave in to defeat.

Once we learn to walk through our paths without stumbling on ourselves, your or my story will be a great footnote in history. Over the years I've managed to comprehend that every successful person has a painful story, and behind every painful story is often a successful ending. Such is the nature of humanity. All we've got to do is accept the pain and get ready to welcome success.

As sure as eggs are eggs, we can truly achieve these incredible stories to inspire and empower people's lives. Our success and victory can undoubtedly bring a vast magnitude of change in this world.

---

84   https://quotefancy.com/quote/871142/Napoleon-Hill-You-can-be-anything-you-want-to-be-if-only-you-believe-with-sufficient.

85   https://www.dailyinspirationalquotes.in/2018/11/dont-limit-your-challenges-challenge-your-limits-jerry-dunn/.

86   Robert Schuller, *Tough Times Never Last but Tough People do* (Orient Paperbacks, India, 2006)

Alex Noble said, "Success is not a place at which one arrives, but rather the spirit with which one undertakes and continues the journey"[87]. We all have this spirit. Let our life stories become a voice that can speak life to the voiceless and a change to all the changes that can be changed.

---

[87] https://www.brainyquote.com/quotes/alex_noble_117604

11

INSPIRATION

The big secret is that there is no secret. Whatever your goal, you can get there if you are willing to work. It is called massive action. Action is the gas in the tank. Without you, the car will not run.
—Marcy Blochowiak

It was Monday morning of 15 January. The day was hazy but bright; a few stubborn patches of clouds floated in the atmosphere as a fresh breeze punctuated the air at Michiru Motel in Lilongwe. The day coincided with the annual national celebrations aimed at rejoicing in the life of one of Malawi's freedom fighters John Chilembwe.

On the other hand, the day was also dominated by the usual petty occurrences. Eloquent words were said as constipated eyes maintained their gruesome contact. Suddenly, a rich conversation struck between a prominent grey-haired man of Asian origin and me.

We discussed several issues ranging from influential to confidential. But as the place grew silent, we decided to move to a better place where we could discuss our issues at greater length. I was astonished by the man's unparalleled eloquence, which struck me with euphoria and positivity. Then, I realised the kind of wisdom that was inborn in this grey-haired man. I took advantage of our meeting to steal some wisdom from him, hoping to quench my thirst for further knowledge.

Through our proceedings, I learnt that our level of influence and capacity to achieve great things is dependent on the nature of the environment we live in. If we are surrounded by average-minded people, we shall be influenced by them. But if we are surrounded by bright sparks, people with eagle vision, we are likely going to prevail in life.

He explained that life is an examination that is passed if we are disciplined and motivated. He said there is a need for people to always have a mission for a vision to be accomplished. He also stressed that we should be enthusiastic about what we intend to achieve.

He noted that people usually do better in things they have a passion for. He explained that confidence in oneself and properly set goals are crucial for success. Above all, he said we should have a burning desire to breathe life into our visions while properly being disciplined in managing our time. After some serious soul searching, I realised that reading good books, having day-to-day experiences, and associating with people with great minds can expand one's knowledge.

On the other hand, what makes people fail is basically attached to what people think about them or related to the place where they live or grew up. Insufficiency and one's social class have nothing to do with preventing people from reaching their highest potential. We are more intelligent and able to surmount any difficult circumstance. We must not allow failure to dominate our lives.

In fact, what we are today is hinged on what we think about ourselves. We must not live by the standards of our present status quo. We must change our mindsets; we must not go to school to get better grades so that we can get white-collar *jobs;* rather, we must go to school to acquire knowledge that can help us to think outside the box. Education should help us think big.

We should aim to become good employers, not better employees, as is the case with most people whose objective for attaining education is to become excellent employees. We must not be impostors of other people's lives or those who follow the crowd; instead, we should seek our own ways of achieving big things in life. We should realise that we are unique; we should be well equipped with skills and beliefs and then do things in our own way.

God created us in a special way, and we can do anything; we should not always use education as the only means of getting employment where we can be good employees. We should think of getting classroom knowledge to become good employers.

We should desist from doing what everybody else can do, and then feel comfortable with that. We must develop our own ways of doing things against traditional methods. We are unique and well-equipped,. so we must make powerful decisions for our own destiny.

The secret that defines our success lies in the kinds of choices and associations we make. Then we should make great decisions. As a part of my approval, I have found the cause of my ignorance.

I admire the grey-haired man not only for his teachings that hinged on principles of success but the fact that, unlike most Asian nationals living in our country, he is a down-to-earth Malawian who owns a business empire with a story we can all learn from. The grey-haired man is Mr Tony Karim, who has financially assisted the most successful businesspeople in Malawi. Besides, this book might not be possible without Mr Karim, from whom I got the inspiration. I look to him as a role model.

In conclusion, what I have acquired through experience is a full set of valuable life skills that freed me from the vicious jaws of poverty. Again, the insights and testimonies I got from Joel Osteen's writings, which my martial arts trainer introduced me to, have helped me draw closer to God and know him better. Thank God, I am safe now.

12

JACK OF ALL TRADES AND MASTER OF ALL

⬤━⬤⬤⬤━⬤

All my life I have learnt to embrace a culture of selflessness through limitlessness.
—Walter Grahams (my teacher! Also well known as Master Nd'o)

⬤━⬤⬤⬤━⬤

As a martial artist, I realise we need to embrace ambitious beliefs, which I strongly believe is key to any successful journey in life. We all have roles to play, not just in improving our own lives but that of others. Generally, when a person succeeds in life, one should also think about people who struggle in order to bring the best out of their lives too. Life is not all about enjoying the grace and glamour; rather, it's about lighting each other's world or giving back to society with what we've been blessed with.

My master's success has now inspired my dreams of developing a boarding school for the underprivileged. The institution would offer academic and martial arts classes to produce a generation of optimistic thinkers and achievers. The most important thing we can do in order to achieve great things is just believe.

The reason I sincerely applaud my master for being a selfless person is solely for the fact that he has seen me climbing to the top of the ladder of success. If it were not for his generosity and kindness, I might have continued languishing with the sting of an empty purpose. The master did everything to show me love and light at the end of the tunnel. He invested his time and resources to mould me into my current shape, making it possible for me to attain academic excellence as well as skills to become a prominent martial artist. My master is one of the rare species whom people of Malawi require.

He is the type to knock down envy, walk tall, and then plant seeds whose generation can bear fruits that can help others succeed. He has lavishly helped me and others without expecting anything in return. Such a big heart!

Africa can be a better place to live in if we empathise with each other. As a country, Malawi may be lagging in various spheres of life, but through supporting each other we can move out of the mess. Generally, most inhabitants of the country lack the spirit of supporting each other. But my master has defied the odds; he is a kind and supportive character who has shaped me to be the man I am today. The master is an icon and the primary source of inspiration not only to me but to others . Being a jack of all trades and master of all, he has broken barriers of selfishness through his lavishness and limitlessness to help direct people to realise their potential and dreams.

Through his inspirational character, I have achieved great things I had never dreamed of. He built and showed me the way to a prosperous life regardless of my background. As someone, who has been supported by others to trace my way to success, I do not fold my arms and keep quiet when things go haywire for other people. I have actually learnt from my master that the human heart is pivotal in making the underprivileged achieve great things and consequently forget their hassles and hurdles.

There is an adage that says no man is an island, meaning every person is malnourished in life, and as such we need others to give us a push. Selfishness and self-praise should not be allowed to be part of our lives, because no matter how famous or how well-heeled one might be, there is a time we shall require others to assist us in one way or another. Death is the best illustration of how we hinge on each other. No matter how famous one is while alive, when death knocks at a person's door, one still needs others to provide them with burial. People just depend on each other. This is the reason I made up my mind to support the less fortunate.

Most of my wishes have materialised not because I have a lot of disposable income but because I have realised that no one climbs the ladder of success alone. There is a need to support each other in order to excel. Bragging about what we have accumulated or achieved cannot make sense to people with insufficient resources. Even God advises us to use the resources we have to benefit others. Our maker says in the Good Book, "Blessed is the hand that gives than the one that receives"[88]. Meaning, that through giving we get blessed. We should learn to give more even from the little we have, without expecting any benefits in return.

One of the ways I have identified to support them is through establishing a special foundation where young ones, especially those who are struggling (vulnerable groups), would be provided with various forms of education. It is only through the provision of education that we can turn people's fortunes in Africa and the world as a whole. Essentially, I believe that every person was blessed with a particular gift or talent, but others fail to realise this potential in order to achieve their dreams; their wishes are nipped in the bud due to a lack of necessary support systems. American talk show host, television producer, author, and actress Oprah Winfrey once said, "Let your light shine within so that it can shine on someone else"[89].

The foundation I am determined to establish would disclose, expose, and nurture hidden talents in most young people, which might help them succeed and lead independent lives. Through such initiatives, I am convinced that we can reduce the number of children loitering in streets for alms or scavenging dump sites where they are exposed to risky lifestyles that pose a danger to their lives. Together we can turn vulnerable children into productive and responsible citizens who can become great leaders just like you and me! Let's join hands to make a difference!

---

[88]   https://www.bucknerkenya.org/blessed-is-the-hand-that-giveth/
[89]   https://www.christianity.com/wiki/bible/what-does-it-mean-to-let-your-light-shine.html?amp=1

13

THE ALPHABET FOR ACTION

Your beliefs determine your actions and your actions
determine your results, but first you must believe.
—Mark Victor Hansen

As an advocate for BELIEVE and a deep thinker, I would like to share an alphabet for action for possibility thinking as adapted from Robert Schuller[90].

A—AFFIRM

We must claim the type of life we wish to lead by becoming the type of person we desire to become.

B—BELIEVE

Have faith that sometime, somewhere, with or without someone's help we can achieve the desires of our hearts.

C—COMMITMENT

We must have a personal statement and make a vow to do everything possible regardless of the situation. We should be strong-minded to thrash fear of failure. Nothing devastates or holds people back more than fear of failure. Anyone who tries to do something great only to fail is not a failure. Failures are people who are knocked out before getting into the ring.

D—DARE

We should defy any possible risks whenever we want to venture into an activity. Dare to believe, dare to commit yourself to something. People who don't take risks can do nothing, have nothing, and will remain nothing.

To live is risking death. To try is risking failure. To believe is risking doubt.

E—EDUCATE

We must teach ourselves not to take shortcuts as others do. The training may be a grind, but those who are too lazy to learn never gain the knowledge they might require, which in turn diminishes their chances of prevailing. Ultimately, knowledgeable people have the right answers to any questions life poses.

F—FIND

We should always try as much as possible to discover our talents, capabilities, time, money, and ways that can help us to fulfil our desires. In accordance with finding what

---

90 Robert Schuller, *Tough Times Never Last but Tough People do* (Orient Paperbacks, India, 2006)

we need to achieve, Proverb 25:2 reads, "It is God's glory to conceal a matter". Just as a diamond is buried deep in the ground, and gold is carefully mined, our talents are found deep within ourselves.

G—GIVE

The attitude of giving is one of the secrets of a successful life. As said in the Bible by apostle Paul, "He who sows sparingly will also reap sparingly and he who sows bountifully will also reap bountifully"[91]. If you want to succeed, go for it, and then give all you have. People who succeed give extra effort and push themselves beyond normal borders.

H—HOPE

Hope is all about trusting in God. Hope is praying and not giving up. If you want to succeed, expect and never quit.

I—IMAGINE

We should let our minds be controlled by positive thoughts. We should imagine crossing the finishing line. We should envisage ourselves climbing mountains to find remedies to our problems.

J—JUNK

We must remove all the useless items from our minds, all the junk stemming from our emotions and thoughts.

K—KNOCKOUT

Let us focus on our thoughts to triumph over depression. We should try as much as possible to win against discouragement and negative thinking. Our minds are extremely important, as what saturates our thoughts shall manifest in our lives.

L—LAUGH

To be a positive thinker and achieve significant success, we must learn to laugh at ourselves and the difficulties we encounter daily.

---

[91]   https://web.mit.edu/jywang/www/cef/bible/NIV/NIV_Bible/2COR+9.html

M—MAKE IT HAPPEN

No matter how intense challenges we face might be, we should always struggle to make things happen.

N—NEGOTIATE

We cannot always have our desires easily met; therefore, we should learn to negotiate and compromise. Be willing to start smaller while focussing on the growth of our plans.

O—OVERLOOK AND OVERCOME

Certain problems won't have quick solutions; it is therefore important to overlook and overcome such problems.

P—PERSEVERE

This is an important word for action. Perseverance is one of the commonest ingredients for success. Winning is not only about being the first and the best in doing things; winning is when we give every bit of our efforts towards what we are doing.

Q—QUIT

We must stop complaining, as life will not always be as blissful as we might anticipate. We must stop concentrating on what we are not, but on what we are focussing on, and then concentrate on what we would like to be.

We should close the previous day's door and then throw the keys away. We should not be frightened of what tomorrow might bring. Instead, we should be content with the day we are in.

R—REORGANISE

Whether we succeed or not, we still need to reorganise ourselves. Reorganisation is pivotal in business and life to experience growth and maturity. We must constantly reorganise ourselves as times are dynamic.

S—SHARE

God can do great things for us if we don't mind who gets the credit or are willing to share. An open mind with a big heart should be willing to share the credit, share the power and share the glory.

T—TRADE-OFF

As a token of appreciation for what God has given us, we must learn to swap what we have for something worthwhile. Trade-off gives joy when we see other people succeeding.

U—UNLOCK

Unlock some human values you have never experienced before, including faith, hope, and love. Let these values be a driving force towards our true success.

V—VISUALISE

We must see in our mind's eye the dreams we have. Don't ever lose the vision. When we lose the vision, we are dead. The Good Book declares that, "Where there is no vision, people perish"[92]. We must set new goals and believe they can be achieved. We must visualise the ultimate success in our lives.

Whatever we envision and intend to achieve, surely we shall have it. If we have a negative vision, we shall reap negative results, yet if we have positive dreams, we shall also get compatible results.

Success starts in our minds. Every person has the freedom to choose to be successful or not. But the best thing we should always desire is to be successful. We must perceive ourselves as successful people, and eventually that shall come to pass.

Visualising success comes from visualising what one would like to be. Success is not determined by the type of environment we are in; generally, it originates from the way we think. Think positively and visualise success.

We need to ask ourselves what we want to accomplish. Then we should ask ourselves if it's indeed necessary to continue with our status. Then we should ask ourselves if we shall be happy with the type of success we are pursuing.

---

92   https://www.churchofjesuschrist.org/study/scriptures/ot/prov/29?lang=eng

W—WORK

As written in Proverbs 14:23 "There is profit in hard work, but mere talk leads to poverty.". There is no substitute for hard work, hard work is crucial for achieving one's goals and that mere talk or empty promises are not enough to achieve success.

X – XRAY

We must live by the creed while 'x-raying' our motives so we can yield it all to God.

Y – YIELD

In the book Romans, Paul says, "Yield yourself unto God". This ostensibly means that as we live in this world, we must work hard to produce good results that should benefit our lives and please God our creator.

Z—ZIP IT UP

We must package everything and then we come to the end and where we can zip it all up with strong determination. Success doesn't come easy; it requires effort, planning, and determination. We must be organized, focused, and committed to achieving our goals.

14

DO NOT LET YOUR CIRCUMSTANCES DEFINE YOU

A person without belief is like a car without an engine—it may
have a beautiful appearance, but it will not get you anywhere. The
stronger the belief, the further and faster you will go.
—Arnold Fox

steemed reader, I thank you for spending your valuable time and effort reading this book, which is an adaptation from my personal experiences which are fruits of the power of belief. I am Yusuf Sabiku, a Malawian national currently in my thirties, married, and living a happy life with my family.

Most people are prone to an inferiority complex, anxiety, tension, or physical, mental, and spiritual ailments that are major causes of poverty in our societies. It is against this background that I have come up with this material, which illustrates the gradual evolution of my thinking. God has blessed me lavishly, and it is my sincere wish that you should also be evacuated from the vicious jaws of poverty and desperation similar to the ones that pinned me down, and then start leading exuberant lives. It is also my hope that this book will help you break the chains of poverty, empower you to a higher mindset, and most importantly, inspire you to dream big.

I grew up in Lilongwe, the capital city of Malawi where I never thought of going to school as I usually loitered in refuse dumping sites with my siblings, collecting various waste materials that we could sell to fend for our family, which rarely afforded daily meals.

Life was a challenge for me due to the numerous hardships I faced. My family was living in extreme poverty and could barely afford the basics, such as three meals a day or decent clothes. I only had one pair of faded black Timberland shoes that my father would repair by cutting up pieces from old tires and gluing them to the soles. I often had to walk barefoot and was the laughingstock among my school peers because of my ragged attire.

My family lived in a two-bedroom house without electricity or running water. Studying at night was nearly impossible because our only source of light was a single improvised kerosene lamp, which was only available during supper. To make matters worse, we couldn't afford to keep the lamp filled with kerosene all the time, so we spent most nights in total darkness. We all shared a single bedroom, with boys on one side of the room and girls on the other, and slept on traditional bare mats with no mattresses or pillows. We improvised pillows from old, dirty clothes, and waking up with body pains from sleeping on a hard surface was a daily occurrence.

We had to fetch water from boreholes since our home had no water supply. Sometimes we woke up at 2.00 or 3.00 in the morning to fetch water ahead of many people in the community, who queued endlessly for the same. Despite these challenges, I persevered, sacrificing everything, including happiness, peers, and pride to focus on my education and personal development, and dream of a better future. Epictetus said, "Circumstances don't make the man, they only reveal him to himself". I firmly believed that my circumstance did not define me, but how I handled them was what mattered.

I was not the brightest in class, but I tried my level best to perform well. I built resilience against life's challenges, including grinding poverty, to remain strong. My optimism for a brighter future never wavered. Indeed, struggle was my lifestyle in those days, but I kept believing that one day I would make it and become a beacon of hope for my family.

On several occasions, I couldn't attend school due to a lack of sustenance, and my academic performance suffered as a result. As such I usually spent my time in video showrooms to get solace through watching movies, but tendrils of poverty stubbornly pulled me back to the realities of life.

Martial arts movies became my darling in the video showrooms. It was at such times and places that my dream of becoming a martial artist was nurtured. At age eight, I came across a martial arts master who spent most of his time training. I wished he could provide me with similar training, but it took me close to a year of persuading him to train me.

By the grace of God, the martial arts master admitted my younger brother and me to the training. He also advised us to enrol at a nearby school where he promised to pay for our tuition as we were put up at his home as children of his own. He highlighted the importance of combining martial arts with education. He explained that acquiring martial arts skills alone without education was like a garden encroached by weeds.

Meanwhile, we mastered the art; we became accomplished, which made us outwit our peers wherever we went. My skills were polished further by reading various publications about martial arts.

Later on, my trainer introduced me to the book *Become a Better You* by Joel Osteen. Through that book I realised that all the years I spent in martial arts training only focused on building a strong mind and body but created a huge deficit in my spirituality.

At that time I didn't have any spiritual inclination or know who Joel Osteen was. The only thing I knew about him was that he was a public speaker and religious writer. The book was marvellous that it instantly changed my perception of life and gave me powerful spiritual growth.

Thereafter, I embraced spirituality and then became a believer. I felt the presence of God in my life wherever I went, which supplemented the levels of strength in my life, to believe in myself and everything I did. The cocoon of doubt in which I was embroiled was finally broken, and then my territory was broadened to what it currently is.

Since then, I understood what my martial arts trainer meant when he told me that martial arts begins with the body, passes on to the mind, and finally settles in the heart. The aspect of perfecting my martial arts skills finally perfected other endeavours of my life. Hitherto, I've realised that the difference between the impossible and the possible lies in our own determination and belief in the self.

I thank God that I finally succeeded in martial arts training and that I am a master with a fourth degree black belt. Besides that, I own a martial arts academy that enrols trainees from different countries.

Through what God has blessed me with I am able to support my family, relatives, and other needy people. Learning the art and becoming transformed is the most wonderful thing that has ever happened in my life. I've always noted that for a person to achieve something great in life, one must toil and face various obstacles, but he or she must overcome them with determination.

If you put limits on everything you do, physical or anything else, it will spread into your work and life. There are no limits. There are only plateaus and you must not stay there, you must go beyond them.

I am certain that our peace of mind or inner peace and the ecstasy we get out of life are dependent not on outside formalities but on harmonisation between our beliefs and dominant thoughts. Consequently, our life as denoted is what our thoughts make it.

What matters is to dare to believe.

15

THE MIRROR EFFECT

The activities of the mind have no limits; they form the surroundings of life. An impure mind surrounds itself with impure things and a pure mind surrounds itself with pure things, just as a picture is drawn by an artist, surroundings are therefore created by the activities of the mind.
—The Buddha

I am a big believer in the mirror test and the effect it encompasses. I strongly encourage you to spare a moment and look in the mirror and then express yourself honestly and tell the person you see. The way we perceive ourselves is what we are, and we shall remain that way. If we view ourselves as successful, that is obviously what we shall be, at the same time bearing in mind that the vice versa might also be true.

Oftentimes, what we envision of ourselves is what we become. Albert Einstein said, "Imagination is everything. It is the preview of life's coming attractions".[93] Get in the habit of creative envisioning. Every time we practice creative envisioning, we must see ourselves as we want to be. We must always have a clear mental picture of ourselves regardless of the opposing forces we face; undoubtedly, sooner or later our imaginations shall become self-fulfilling prophecies.

The magic of visualisation should unmistakably be used in all situations to enhance the development of our inner person that shall be seen outwardly. The philosophy behind the mirror effect entails that if we aspire for greatness, be it in the spiritual or physical realm, if that's what we truly want, all we need to do is envision ourselves embracing and enjoying that moment as it has already been manifested upon our lives. Like a mirror, life will reflect what a person thinks about it.

I was fortunate to have a mentor in my life like my martial arts teacher; everything he taught me has proven to be helpful and worthwhile today.

I hope that sharing these thoughts with you will provide you with guidance as well as inspiration. I foresee a world where all people are inspired to believe in themselves and their capabilities as well as empowered to possibilities, able to potentialise, and to realise all their dreams. Let my life be a window for your radiance to shine through and a mirror to reflect tenderness and tranquillity to all of humanity.

This book is an indication of a collective thought process that I believe can lead people to the type of success they dream of. Through continuous visualisation and hard work, miracles have been created for me, and it might likewise do the same for you if its contents are devoured and properly digested and acted upon with belief.

You hear and you forget. You see and you remember. You do and you will understand.

On your way in search of wisdom, you will encounter great books. Some you will come across are meant to be tasted, some are meant to be chewed, and some are meant to be

---

93   https://www.brainyquote.com/quotes/albert_einstein_384440.

swallowed. I would hope that the contents of this book will be swallowed wholeheartedly in order to satisfy and quench your hunger for knowledge and thirst for enlightenment.

Most importantly, may this book help you to be

Blessed and Enthusiastic with Limitless and Incomparable Eminence in Victory and Enlightenment. BELIEVE!

Adieu!

Printed in the United States
by Baker & Taylor Publisher Services